Praise for *Reach for Greatness*

Yong Zhao again provokes and challenges our thinking by sounding a call to immediate action. Our education system must fundamentally change to meet the needs of our children. With insightful personal stories and penetrating analysis of our current education system, Zhao, at once challenging, provocative, and optimistic, shows us that personalizable education models are the way to transform our education system from one that supports mediocrity to one which magnifies the passions and talents of each student.

—Rod Allen
Superintendent, Cowichan Valley School District
Former Assistant Deputy Minister of Education
British Columbia, Canada

A bold and compelling call for a wholesale shift in our education priorities. With powerful stories and examples, Dr. Zhao lays out an aspirational goal for our schools: empower each child to create a distinctive path to greatness by reinforcing strengths and unleashing passions. Read this, and you'll be inspired!

—Ted Dintersmith
Author of *What School Could Be*
Executive Producer of the Documentary *Most Likely to Succeed*

Reach for Greatness *is a must-read for the truly professional educator today. Common sense and expert practice are hard to find. Yong Zhao brings insight and intelligence in arguing for a dramatic shift of thinking about schooling that is fit for today's world. This book helps give shape to a robust narrative sorely needed for every student.*

—Greg Whitby
Executive Director of Schools, Diocese of Parramatta, Australia
Author of *Educating Gen Wi-Fi*

Are you keen for the real depth and substance of an education that helps all students to reach their full potential but tired of empty promises for "personalized learning"? If so, Yong Zhao's Reach for Greatness *is the book for you! With vivid examples and carefully scaffolded argumentation, Zhao shows how what he calls "personalizable education" offers an exciting and practical future for all of our students truly to become great. Zhao's writing is so full of whimsy and humor that you can't wait to see what this wonderful alchemist of educational change is going to say next. Best of all, this gem of a book is one that not only all teachers, but also a rising generation of students, will cherish.*

—Dennis Shirley
Professor, Lynch School of Education, Boston College
Editor-in-Chief, *Journal of Educational Change*

Reading a book by Yong Zhao is always an educational awakening! In Reach for Greatness, *Zhao makes it clear that students are the potential for greatness within schools, not a problem our educational system needs to fix. This book challenges educators to re-examine the true purpose of education and commit to supporting students' passions and cultivating their strengths. Personalizable education occurs when students are in the driver's seat—their voices need to be heard, valued, and acted upon. Thanks to Zhao, I am more determined than ever to ensure that students are not just along for the ride.*

—Russell J. Quaglia
Author of *Teacher Voice, Parent Voice,
Student Voice,* and *Aspire High*

Yong Zhao, ever the engaging education contrarian, delivers a compelling read that systematically outlines how to break away from educational systems that narrow, dictate, and sort learners, and readjust to focus on students' unique skills, needs, and passions. It brings the role of education—in society and for the individual—to the forefront and, in doing so, has the reader reappraise its purpose. Moving beyond just a recommendation of personalization, Zhao promotes the idea of education personalized by, not for, the learner.

—Sean Slade
Senior Director of Global Outreach, ASCD

Yong Zhao pulls us from our narrow view of what education is and reminds us what it needs to be. Personalized education (as opposed to the ubiquitous and limited notion of personalized learning) is essential for recognizing and cultivating the diverse strengths of our students for their own good and the good of society. Poignant stories from Zhao's global travels to schools make the research in this call to action relatable and accessible for all educational stakeholders. This is an important read!

—Emily McCarren
Academy Principal, Punahou School
Co-Author of The Take Action Guide to
World Class Learners book series

In Reach for Greatness, *Yong Zhao makes the urgent case for empowering every young person to recognize their strengths, realize their talents, and follow their passions. Furthermore, his idea of empowerment is centered on the young person taking control of their own learning—a critical shift from the dominant model in which education is done to the student. Clear, compelling, evidence-based, and practical, this is an important book.*

—Ross Hall
Director of Education, Ashoka
Founder, The Global Change Leaders

Reach for Greatness

Corwin Impact Leadership Series

Series Editor: Peter M. DeWitt

Forthcoming contributions from Andy Hargreaves and Alma Harris

Reach for Greatness
Personalizable Education for All Children

Yong Zhao

A SAGE Publishing Company

FOR INFORMATION:

Corwin

A SAGE Company

2455 Teller Road

Thousand Oaks, California 91320

(800) 233-9936

www.corwin.com

SAGE Publications Ltd.

1 Oliver's Yard

55 City Road

London EC1Y 1SP

United Kingdom

SAGE Publications India Pvt. Ltd.

B 1/I 1 Mohan Cooperative Industrial Area

Mathura Road, New Delhi 110 044

India

SAGE Publications Asia-Pacific Pte. Ltd.

3 Church Street

#10-04 Samsung Hub

Singapore 049483

Publisher: Arnis Burvikovs

Content Development Editor: Desirée A. Bartlett

Editorial Assistant: Eliza Riegert

Production Editor: Amy Schroller

Copy Editor: Liann Lech

Typesetter: C&M Digitals (P) Ltd.

Proofreader: Christine Dahlin

Indexer: Amy Murphy

Cover Designer: Michael Dubowe

Printed in the United States of America

ISBN 978-1-5063-1609-3

This book is printed on acid-free paper.

Certified Chain of Custody
Promoting Sustainable Forestry
www.sfiprogram.org
SFI-01268

SFI label applies to text stock

18 19 20 21 22 10 9 8 7 6 5 4 3 2 1

Contents

Acknowledgments

I owe many people a debt of gratitude for making this book possible. First, I want to thank my parents for not insisting on improving my farming skills when I was growing up. Although farming seemed the only destiny for me at the time and I was worse than inadequate at managing the water buffalo, my parents let me run away from the apparent deficit by allowing me to go to school, where I found my strengths and confidence. Second, I am grateful for all the teachers in my life for forgiving my apparent weaknesses and supporting my exploration of my interests and strengths. I have been extremely fortunate to have many caring and forgiving teachers in my life, in particular, Teachers Hu and Tang in elementary school, Teacher Wang in middle school, Teachers Jiang and Long in high school and Dr. Gary Cziko in graduate school. These teachers and my parents made it possible for me to author this book about strength-based education. In some way, they created a personalizable education for me.

I am deeply grateful for the courageous and inspiring work of numerous educators and students. It is through interactions with them that I developed the ideas in this book. Their work not only reinforced my belief in the urgent need for personalizable education but also convinced me that such an education is possible. While it is impossible to name all the educators and students who shaped my thinking, I must acknowledge a few who have contributed a great deal to this book. Peter Hutton, principal of Templestowe College in Australia, made it possible for me to observe personalizable education in action. Chris Aviles, EdTech Coach at Fair Haven schools in New Jersey, and Mark Suter, computer science teacher at

Elida High School in Ohio, shared with me their innovative work and impact on students. I must also thank John Cahalin and his colleagues at Real World Scholars for their work with teachers and students to build authentic classroom-based enterprises, from which I drew much inspiration.

The book also benefited directly from the work I have been doing through the Mitchell Institute at Victoria University, in particular the Paradigm Shifters project that put into practice some of the ideas included in this book. The project was implemented in partnership with Victorian Association of State Secondary Principals and New South Wales Secondary Principals Council. Sara Glover, Michelle Anderson, Chris Cawsey, Judy Crowe, Wayne Perkins, and Dianne Hennessy were instrumental in making the project possible. Likewise, I learned a great deal from the Rudolph project with the Association of Independent Schools in South Australia under the leadership of Carolyn Grantskalns and Mary Hudson. The Rudolph project also put to test some of the ideas discussed in the book. The principals, teachers, and students participated in these projects helped me refine many of the ideas that appear in this book.

Finally, I am grateful for the many encouraging and insightful conversations with my editor, Arnis Burvikovs at Corwin. As always, Arnis's gentle reminders and thoughtful feedback made the final product significantly better.

While the book has benefited from the contribution of many, all errors are mine.

—Yong Zhao
Lawrence, Kansas
October 3, 2017

About the Author

Yong Zhao is a Foundation Distinguished Professor in the School of Education at the University of Kansas. He is also a professorial fellow at the Mitchell Institute for Health and Education Policy, Victoria University in Australia, as well as a Global Chair at the University of Bath, UK. He previously served as the Presidential Chair and Director of the Institute for Global and Online Education in the College of Education, University of Oregon, where he was also a Professor in the Department of Educational Measurement, Policy, and Leadership. Before joining Oregon, Yong Zhao was University Distinguished Professor at the College of Education, Michigan State University, where he also served as the founding director of the Center for Teaching and Technology, executive director of the Confucius Institute, as well as the US-China Center for Research on Educational Excellence.

Yong Zhao's works focus on the implications of globalization and technology on education. He has published over 100 articles and

30 books, including *Counting What Counts: Reframing Education Outcomes* (2016), *Never Send a Human to Do a Machine's Job: Correcting Top 5 Ed Tech Mistakes* (2015), *Who's Afraid of the Big Bad Dragon: Why China has the Best (and Worst) Education System in the World* (2014), *Catching Up or Leading the Way: American Education in the Age of Globalization* (2009) and *World Class Learners: Educating Creative and Entrepreneurial Students* (2012).

Yong Zhao has received numerous awards, including the Early Career Award from the American Educational Research Association, Outstanding Public Educator from Horace Mann League of USA, and Distinguished Achievement Award in Professional Development from the Association of Education Publishers. He is an elected fellow of the International Academy for Education and is recognized as one of the most influential education scholars.

Introduction

Stop Looking at My Bad Leg

Benjamin Franklin wrote about a philosopher friend of his who used his two legs to determine with whom to avoid acquaintances more than 200 years ago. In "The Deformed and Handsome Leg," Franklin says there are two kinds of people: One always finds beauty and good in things and people and thus is happy and pleasant to be with, while the other always looks for the contrary and thus is unhappy and unpleasant all the time. Franklin advises that we should stay away from the latter at all costs. To determine the kind of people in a stranger, Franklin's friend noted the stranger's reaction to his legs. Franklin's friend had one "remarkably handsome" leg and "the other by some accident crooked and deformed. If a Stranger at the first Interview, regarded his ugly Leg more than his handsome one, he doubted him. If he spoke of it, and took no Notice of the handsome Leg, that was sufficient to determine my Philosopher to have no farther Acquaintance with him" (Franklin, 1780).

Unfortunately, most children do not have the same luxury as Franklin's philosopher friend to decide whether they want to continue the acquaintance with such an unpleasant character. Education today is very much like the stranger who keeps looking at Franklin's friend's ugly leg more than his handsome one. It is obsessed with what children do not know or are unable to do. Worse, education today has developed various ways to speak about children's deficiency, publicly and loudly, in the forms of tracking, grade retention, and sorting into different programs such as special education, summer remediation, and extra tutoring. It goes even beyond talking about children's presumed deficiencies; education today works very hard to fix them, ignoring and potentially harming the handsome leg.

What made education such an unpleasant character is the gap mindset. The primary mission of education, as believed by many, is to instill in all children a set of knowledge and skills at a similar pace. This set of knowledge and skills, usually codified as curriculum standards, is presumed to be necessary for successful living in a society. To ensure all children are equipped with the prescribed skills and knowledge at the same pace, education has developed an elaborate system of assessments and checkpoints. Children are regularly (and frequently) assessed against the standards so as to detect and hopefully remedy any gaps.

Of course, gaps exist. Students' mastery of the knowledge and skills, measured by standardized tests, varies a great deal. Some students seem to excel, while others lag behind. But for a variety of reasons, it has been found that groups of students with certain backgrounds as a whole seem to lag behind other groups. For example, in the United States, students from low-income families are less likely than their wealthier peers to demonstrate that they have achieved the prescribed standards. Similarly, ethnic minority students, particularly African American and Hispanic students, score lower than their Caucasian counterparts on standardized tests.

The gaps have received much attention around the world. Dubbed achievement gaps, many societies have enacted major policies and invested massive resources to close them. The United States is a prime example.

THE ACHIEVEMENT GAP MANIA IN AMERICA

For nearly two decades, since the enactment of the No Child Left Behind Act of 2001 (NCLB) (No Child Left Behind Act of 2001, 2002) in 2002, America has been suffering from "achievement gap mania" (Hess, 2011). Closing the achievement gap has been the commanding, almost exclusive, goal of education in America. All educational efforts, be they in policy, research, or practice, must be justified on the grounds that they can help close the achievement gap. As a result, the nation has devoted all its educational resources to the campaign to narrow the chasm in test scores and graduation rates between students of different backgrounds, particularly in income and race.

The campaign has been a futile one. The gap between the poor and the rich has not narrowed significantly, nor has the chasm between children of color and their White counterparts (Annie E. Casey Foundation, 2013; Curran & Kellogg, 2016; Plucker, Hardesty, & Burroughs, 2013)—in fact, it has widened (Ostashevsky, 2016; Reardon, 2011). The drastic policies put forth by NCLB, the billions of dollars, the numerous instructional innovations, and the tireless efforts of educators did not seem to have turned schools into an effective mechanism to alter the trajectory preset by children's family background before they arrive at school. Today, factors associated with a child's home remain much more powerful predictors of their future than do schools (Annie E. Casey Foundation, 2010; Bailey & Dynaski, 2011; Curran & Kellogg, 2016; Duncan & Murnane, 2011; Fryer & Levitt, 2004; Reardon, 2011).

Worse, the campaign has been counterproductive (Hess, 2011). Beyond the squandered resources and opportunities, "achievement gap mania" has significantly changed American education for the worse. It

> has led to education policy that has shortchanged many children. It has narrowed the scope of schooling. It has hollowed out public support for school reform. It has stifled educational innovation. It has distorted the way we approach educational choice, accountability, and reform. (Hess, 2011)

It has also turned American education into test preparation, resulting in massive "collateral damages" (Nichols & Berliner, 2007). It has demoralized educators and students (Nichols & Berliner, 2008; Smith & Kovacs, 2011; Wong, Wing, & Martin, 2016), and it has deprived many children, particularly those whom the campaign was supposed to help, of the opportunities for a real education (Carter & Welner, 2013; Tienken & Zhao, 2013). Furthermore, it has reinforced the deficit mindset for minority students and concealed the real cause for educational inequality (Cross, 2007; Jones, 2013; Ladson-Billings, 2007).

Nevertheless, the campaign continues. The well-evidenced failure and damaging consequences of efforts summoned by NCLB to narrow the achievement gaps have apparently not caused American policymakers to change course. Although NCLB was replaced by the Every Student Succeeds Act (ESSA) in 2015 (Every Student Succeeds Act, 2015–2016), closing the achievement gaps remains the commanding goal of education. Despite the mechanical changes, the purpose of the new education law "is to provide all children significant opportunity to receive a fair, equitable, and high-quality education, and to close educational achievement gaps" (Every Student Succeeds Act, 2015–2016, Section 1001). Barring any significant changes, achievement gap mania will continue to reign over American education for the foreseeable future.

RUDOLPH AND ME

Rudolph had a red nose. It is a deficit because the standard nose color is supposed to be black in reindeer country. So all efforts were applied to fix his nose color. And, of course, the poor red-nosed reindeer was not normal and did not meet the standard. The other reindeers with black noses were the good ones and did not want to mix with the bad kid. But all the children around the world should be grateful that no one fixed Rudolph's red nose because his red nose was the very thing Santa Claus needed for his sleigh on a foggy Christmas Eve.

I am grateful that no one tried to fix my deficits either. I am able to write this book not because I had planned to be a professor in the United States, but because I was not forced to fix my lack of ability and interest in becoming a farmer in China. I was born in a Chinese village and thus destined to become a farmer like everyone else in the village. But from a very early age, I discovered that I was not cut out to be a successful farmer. I was physically smaller and weaker than other boys. I could not drive water buffalos or climb trees or manipulate the hoe nearly as well as other boys. I tried to learn, and my father was a good teacher, but I was unable to master the farming skills. By any standard, I was way below the average of all the boys in terms of farming knowledge and abilities. There was a clear achievement gap in farming capabilities between me and the other boys in the village.

Luckily, my father did not try too hard to close my achievement gap. He gave up on me early. Instead of pushing me to become a better farmer, he sent me to school. In school, I discovered what I could be good at. My ability to handle reading was much better than my ability to deal with a water buffalo. After all, I could be good at something. And I liked that feeling. However, no one, including my father and myself, knew how I could make a living without farming at the time, when China was in the midst of a disastrous political campaign called the Great Cultural Revolution. The campaign dismantled the formal education system and sent the educated elite to remote rural areas to be "reeducated" by farmers. Education was thus not a way to get out of the village for a better life, like it is today. In other words, it was not the remote chance that education would bring a better life that motivated me to go to school. Instead, it was the feeling that I could be good at something, and the desire to avoid doing something I was not good at, that sustained my motivation to walk barefoot to school every day, in burning summers and freezing winters.

I am a big fan of the "growth mindset" (Dweck, 2008). I strongly believe that anyone can learn anything. But I have tried not to apply the idea to everything in life. I have avoided applying a growth mindset in football, for example, although I know if I indeed put 10,000 hours into it, as Malcolm Gladwell (2008) suggests in his book *Outliers: The Story of Success*, I could become better. But I also know very well that even if I put 100,000 hours into it, I will not be playing for the NFL because my 5'6" height and 150 lb. weight are way below the average height and weight of NFL players. No matter how hard I try, I probably won't get there.

I have also avoided applying it in other undertakings. I gave up on putting 10,000 hours into painting quickly after I discovered that I could barely draw a straight line and the Chinese characters I produced always looked like the footprints of a chicken. I gave up studying math in high school because I did not enjoy math and I was not good at it. I received 3 points out of 120 in the College Entrance Exam in 1982.

I was able to go to college without studying math because of a policy that forgave my poor math performance. In the late 1970s and early 1980s, when Chinese education was recovering from the damages of the Cultural Revolution, it allowed students to major in foreign languages without being good at math. Math was not counted toward the total score of the College Entrance Exam for those applying to study foreign languages. To run away from my poor math, I chose to major in English in college. I was lucky because the policy ended in 1982. Math has since become a required core subject in the College Entrance Exam, which means Chinese students can no longer run away from math if they want to go to college.

I have been fortunate to be able to avoid virtually everything that I have no potential for being good at or I am not interested in. More important, I have been fortunate to have had the space to explore my passions and experiment with different undertakings to discover my weaknesses and strengths. Most people are not born knowing what they are interested in and can be good at. They can only find out through experiences.

But experiences have costs and risks. Every experience requires time, and some require money and extra effort. Thus, adults want every activity their children experience to be positive, to lead to some desirable outcome. They don't want their children to waste their time, energy, or money, or worse, to have experiences that may have a negative impact. Responsible adults naturally have a tendency to prescribe experiences for children. The result is that many children are allowed to have only experiences deemed to be beneficial and safe by adults.

I was fortunate to have broader and more diverse experiences than most children. Although my experiences were severely constrained by the lack of resources and remoteness of my village, I enjoyed more freedom. As soon as I started school, my illiterate parents did not feel they could guide me anymore and thus allowed me to pursue whatever I thought appropriate throughout my life. My teachers in the village school were not well trained to make me follow a prescribed reading curriculum, so I was able to read anything I could find instead of a series of carefully selected graded reading materials. The assortment of used books, magazines, and newspapers my father collected for wrapping noodles in the village noodle factory not only taught me to read but also, more importantly, exposed me to a broad range of topics, way beyond what a very carefully designed curriculum can offer.

Neither my parents nor my teachers attempted to force me to do things they wanted or forbid me from doing things they did not like. I was free of external judgment and never feared it. So I got to have many different experiences, some more beneficial than others, but all were necessary for me to find my passion and strengths. In college, instead of devoting my energy to studying the English textbooks in the classroom, I spent more time reading English books and magazines on psychology, linguistics, and education. Rather than spending time memorizing English literature as required, I took on computer programming. Instead of worrying about my grades, I spent a tremendous amount of time programming a piece of statistics software for a research project. In the end, I developed great proficiency in English by not following the prescribed program.

I have learned to be very open to new experiences. I have always been willing to explore new opportunities. When opportunities present themselves, I jump right in as long as they look interesting, but I am not one who would keep at it at any cost when I realize that it is not something I can be great at or enjoy doing. For example, I tried making fish tanks after college but gave it up when I discovered I have no talent in engineering. I quit being a college teacher to join a translation business, but gave it up despite its success because I did not find it interesting. I returned to be a college teacher afterwards because I found that that was ultimately what interested me.

I was lucky on two fronts. First, I was lucky that my parents and schools did not force me to fix my weaknesses according to whatever their definitions of strengths or weaknesses were. They were very forgiving of my weaknesses and appreciative of my various adventures. Second, I was lucky that the massive societal transformations in China and the world over the past few decades made it possible for me to use my strengths and interests, just as the fog on Christmas Eve made it possible for Rudolph to change his fate. If China had not restored its education system after the Cultural Revolution, it would not have been possible for me to go to college. If China had not opened to the outside world, it would not have been possible for me to migrate to the United States. If I had stayed in China, my passions and strengths would not have found as much value.

Fortunately, the changes I experienced in China are now widespread for everyone. In other words, the foggy Christmas has arrived for all due to technological changes. But unfortunately, the accidental great educational experiences I had are not widespread. To enable every child to be able to explore, experiment with, and enhance his or her strengths, education must change.

THE FOGGY CHRISTMAS EVE HAS ARRIVED

The fundamental reason for people to worry about achievement gaps stems from two assumptions underlying education today. First, there is a set of skills and knowledge everyone must have in order to live a successful life in the world. Second, all children are capable of and interested in acquiring the skills and knowledge at a similar pace. Thus, if a child is found to be behind others, we must act to help him or her catch up at any cost.

These assumptions are not true any longer. First, changes in society always redefine the value of knowledge and skills. What used to be useful can become useless and what used to be useless can become useful, as the experience of Rudolph and me suggests. Given recent changes brought about by technology, there has been growing recognition that traditionally valued skills and knowledge have become obsolete, and we need new human qualities for the new world (Florida, 2012; Partnership for 21st Century Skills, 2007; Pink, 2006; Trilling & Fadel, 2009; Zhao, 2016a).

Second, current understandings of human nature and human learning suggest that human beings are differently talented (Gardner, 1983, 2006) and have different desires and interests (Reiss, 2000, 2004). Thanks to the diversity in the environment in which they are born, humans also have different experiences that interact with their natural talents and interests to give each person a unique, jagged profile of abilities and desires, stronger in some areas and weaker in others (Ridley, 2003; Rose, 2016). In other words, everyone has a handsome leg and, at the same time, a deformed leg.

Third, in the new world where smart technology has replaced and will continue to replace humans in routine tasks, we need human beings to be unique, creative, and entrepreneurial (Schwab, 2015; Wagner, 2008, 2012; World Economic Forum, 2016). Thus, to succeed in the world, we need an education that helps everyone to become uniquely creative and entrepreneurial. Education needs to stop preparing students to become a homogenous group of average individuals—mediocre at everything but great at nothing—and to begin helping everyone to become great.

Greatness comes from lots of efforts (Coyle, 2009), but it can only be built on passion and strengths. If a person has no interest in a domain, it is unlikely that he or she would be intrinsically motivated to put in the necessary efforts needed for greatness. If a person spends the same effort on developing abilities in domains where he or she has neither talent nor rich resources, he or she is unlikely to become great either. Thus, an education that aims to cultivate greatness needs to be one that supports passion and enhances strengths, instead of fixing deficits or closing gaps. It is time to stop looking at the bad leg!

PLAN OF THE BOOK

This book is about teaching for greatness. Chapter 1 discusses why education has been led to ignore passion and strengths. Chapter 2 makes the argument, based on current understanding of human abilities, that every child can be great. It also brings in research from different disciplines to show where strengths and passions can be found. In Chapter 3, I discuss humans' need to become great in order to achieve peace with themselves and arrive at authentic happiness. Chapter 4 argues that in order to teach for greatness, we need to make education personalizable. Differing from personalized learning fundamentally, personalizable education gives students control over their own learning. Features of personalizable education are also discussed. In the last chapter, Chapter 5, I discuss what is needed to realize personalizable education for all children.

CHAPTER
1

The Ambitious Pursuit of Mediocrity

How Education Curtails Children's Potential for Greatness

Hanqing Liu was set up as an example of the disastrous consequences of pursuing one's passion by a Chinese newspaper in 2017. According to a widely circulated story first published in *Yangtse Evening* (Wang, 2017), a local newspaper in Nanjing, China, Liu was admitted to one of the most prestigious and competitive universities in 1980 at the age of 16. At a time when less than 4 percent of high school graduates could be admitted to colleges in China, it is not an exaggeration for Liu, from a poor village, to be viewed as a prodigy. But now, at the age of 53, Liu is living off government welfare in the rural village that had expected him to achieve great accomplishments four decades ago.

Liu was ruined by his passion, the story implies. He was an excellent student for the first two years in college. His life took a downward turn his junior year when he accidentally read a story about one of the best-known Chinese mathematicians who successfully advanced research on Goldbach's conjecture. Mathematically talented, Liu found a passion in mathematics and decided to devote all his time and energy to the study of number theory. He became so obsessed with the beautiful world of numbers that eating and sleeping became a waste of time. He cut his sleep to two hours a day, and he neglected his real major, heat treatment. He did not follow the advice of his mentor and department chair to drop his passion or wait until after graduation because he believed in his passion and that he could become a great mathematician. He failed a number of required courses in his senior year and was given an extra year to make up, but eventually, he did not complete his degree. Thus, he was not assigned a job by the government, which automatically granted jobs to all college graduates in the 1980s. He had to return to his village.

For the next thirty years, Liu continued his research on number theory from his impoverished village home. He never left his village again. He's never been married and never worked beside his research. He wrote a few papers, but none has been published or recognized. He now lives on government welfare, which gives him about 400 yuan (about $60) a month.

After thirty years of pursuing his passion, Liu has accomplished nothing: no farming skills, no children, no wife, no career, no publication, and no money. He is definitely not the great mathematician he wanted to become. He is indeed the poster child of what not to do in life. At the end of the story, the editor reflects, "Pursuing dreams does not mean one should be entirely isolated from reality and completely immersed in one's own world."

The story came out just a few days before the annual Chinese National College Entrance Exam was to take place. It seems to be a warning to the millions of students who were about to go to college of the dangers of pursuing one's passion with perseverance. The story went viral on Chinese social media almost instantly.

VICTIM OF EDUCATION

I would not be surprised that many Chinese parents and teachers would heed the warning and use this story to tell their children and students not to pursue their passions. Many would consider Liu a miserable failure and blame his perceived failure on his own stubbornness and unrealistic pursuit. But I am not sure Liu's life is a failure, as he might have enjoyed his life in the beautiful world of mathematics considerably more than heat treatment engineers who live a more normal life.

More important, the real lesson from Liu's story is not the danger of pursuing one's passion, but how education punishes and curtails human potentials to be great. Liu, with his passion, talent, and perseverance, could well have become a great mathematician with the proper support and resources. While history cannot be undone, we can imagine a completely different fate for Liu. If his mentor and department chair believed that Liu was mathematically talented and found value in his passion, they could have encouraged him to change his major to mathematics or enabled him to transfer to a math program. If he had been able to study as a math major, he could have become one of the best students and not failed college. If he had successfully completed college with a major in math, he could have been given a job working on math. If he had been given a job working on math, he would have had access to experts and resources, including math journals and books he needed to advance his research (none existed in his village). If he had had access to other math researchers and resources, his research could have been significant and then he would have had access to outlets to share his research findings, which could have helped him refine his ideas and advance more. As a result, he could have become a great mathematician with groundbreaking discoveries at best. At worst, he could have lived as a decent professional mathematician.

None of the "ifs" happened to Liu. He was deemed a failure because he did not do what the education system wanted him to do. But he should not be viewed as a victim of his passion; rather, he is a victim of an education that does not reward passion or potential for greatness.

GREATNESS DENIED

Liu's story took place in China, but it can happen anywhere in the world. Admittedly, due to differences in culture and educational systems, it happens with more or less frequency in different societies. For example, American universities are generally more flexible and diverse than the Chinese system. They allow much more flexibility in changing majors of study, which gives people like Liu the possibility of switching into an area of his passion. Moreover, America as a society has more resources and is more likely to give second chances, which enables people who do not fit in the system at one time to bounce back or succeed in other ways. This is why there are more successful people who "failed" college but became great innovators and entrepreneurs in the United States than in China.

However, the success of Steve Jobs, Bill Gates, and Mark Zuckerberg does not conceal the fact that many more people with the potential to become as great fail to realize their potential, even in America. Jobs, Gates, and Zuckerberg are all fortunate to have been born into the right families and communities. They had the good luck to have the right neighbors, teachers, and friends. They happened to be able to choose the right schools as well. Most children in America do not have similar good fortune to be allowed to pursue their passion. Even the few materially privileged or the so-called best and brightest end up as "excellent sheep," spending all their resources and energy going through a process to amass excellent test scores and gold stars to be admitted to elite colleges and doing the same to graduate, as an ex-Yale English professor writes in his book *The Excellent Sheep: The Miseducation of the American Elite and the Way to a Meaningful Life* (Deresiewicz, 2015). They become excellent students but never realize the potential commensurate with their talents, efforts, resources, and sufferings.

The efforts and sufferings students go through in order to become excellent sheep is shocking (Gleason, 2017). Psychologist David

Gleason documents the strenuous and stressful process students in selective schools go through in order to be "excellent" enough to be admitted to elite colleges. He also documents the sacrifices students and their families make for the same process. If the efforts and sacrifices were applied to pursue their strengths and passions, the students could achieve much more than just getting into an elite college.

MANUFACTURED FAILURES

The fate of less privileged children can be even worse. It's not just that their passions and talents may never get discovered and nurtured so they can become great; they are also subject to a constant and systematic assault on their confidence and self-esteem because they are academically behind, as judged by some external standards and tests. They are reminded all the time, through test scores, remediation programs, grade retention, or denial of a high school diploma, that they are failures. Australian journalist Lucy Clark writes about her daughter's heartbreaking story of being a failure in a contribution to the *Guardian* (Clark, 2014):

> Over the two years of her higher school certificate, she has truanted frequently, she has failed to hand in assignments, she has failed to turn up on time, she has failed to meet uniform requirements, she has failed to attend some of her HSC trial exams, she has exhausted the patience of teachers and pushed to the outer limits the structural sympathies of the public school system.

This is after many attempts at intervention and help that included "innumerable official letters outlining her many misdemeanors" and "programs of improvement, second chances, third chances, and more." Expulsion was also proposed. The sense of failure has resulted in tremendous struggle for the teachers; parents; and, of course, Clark's daughter:

> Every day of my daughter's high school life has been a struggle. She wakes up in the morning and the thought of going to school—sometimes even the thought of going outside—is

like an enormous mountain to climb. Very often she hasn't been able to scale it.

There have been times when she just hasn't made it all the way to school: she sits in a park on her own, wondering why she finds it all so hard while her friends trundle on ahead in their "normality"; she has been doubled up in a laneway near the school crying, riveted by her anxiety.

When she has made it there, sitting in class for the duration of a lesson is the next mountain in the range. Anxious thoughts crowd out her bandwidth, blocking the admission of any useful information the teacher might be trying to impart. She told me once in a moment of rare vulnerability that she felt so distressed about being so behind in her classwork that she spent the whole period fighting the urge to flee and throw herself onto the train tracks.

Apparently, Clark's story struck a chord with many parents. Her piece, "My Daughter, My Beautiful Failure," became a popular read, and she expanded it into a popular book, *Beautiful Failures: How the Quest for Success Is Harming Our Kids* (Clark, 2016). Clark's daughter is certainly a failure as judged by the existing education system, which is also responsible for making her a failure. But is she really a failure? Or, more importantly, could she have succeeded in other areas? Does she have other talents and passions that can make her great? Apparently, yes. Besides resilience, Clark writes about her daughter:

> While she has missed just about every mark on the schoolwork journey, she is highly functioning in her social life. . . . What could be more important than succeeding at your personal relationships? Don't we say that at the end?

EDUCATION'S BIG LIE

"Become who you are," "be yourself," "follow your heart," "discover yourself," "reach your full potential," and "find your passion" are among the most common bits of advice given to children by motivational speakers and educators. Many schools put in their promotional materials that they are all about helping children find their passion and realize their potential. Even government education policies talk about providing opportunities to help children reach their full potential. Teachers and parents are constantly told to have high expectations for each and every child.

But in reality, the education system rarely cares about the children's individual passions or talents. The only passion it cares about is the passion to become a good student. The only talent it values is the talent in being a good student: following school rules, doing homework, sitting and listening to whatever is taught, getting good grades, acing all tests, and never questioning the meaning and value of what they are asked to learn and do in school.

With very few exceptions, schools generally do not ask what students are good at, interested in, or passionate about. They do not allocate resources based on students' talents or passions. Virtually all resources are allocated to implement the predetermined, predefined curriculum in order to meet the requirements of the government or other governing bodies. The majority of schools do not provide any significant financial resources to support student-initiated programs out of their regular budgets, nor do they provide time out of the regular school day for students to pursue their talents or passions. While a growing number of schools have begun to implement programs such as genius hours and makerspaces to support students' pursuit of their interests, these programs are fairly limited in scale and reach.

Worse, the current education system actively suppresses individual talents and passions by defining what educational success means and convincing students, parents, and the public to accept the definition. It first convinces people that the skills and knowledge prescribed in the curriculum are the only things worth learning, the only things that lead to life's success. Talents and passions outside the prescribed curriculum may be nice to have, but they won't lead to success in life. Then it constantly measures how children are doing against the preset expectations in the curriculum. Thus, the current definition of education success for individual children is measured by how well *they make the system think* that they have mastered the knowledge and skills the system wants them to learn, through grades and tests. Making the system believe that they have learned something is not necessarily the same as them having actually learned something because grades can simply be about sitting time, good (compliant) behavior in class, completing homework as required, and passing exams. And passing exams does not necessarily mean children have actually learned something, either, because the quality of exams varies.

Children often have to forgo their own interests and talents in order to spend their time on the knowledge and skills that will make them successful. This is especially true for those who are not particularly talented in school subjects or interested in getting good scores, like Lucy Clark's daughter. Children who do not have the good fortune to have access to resources that help them become good at the prescribed subjects are even more likely to have to give up their passions and talents because they have to devote time to "catch up" to their peers.

THE AMBITIOUS PURSUIT OF MEDIOCRITY

The reason for blaming Liu's pursuit of passion for his failed life is the same as the reason for the manufactured failures like Lucy Clark's daughter. It is also the same as the cause of the production of the "excellent sheep." It is the ambitious pursuit of mediocrity, which characterizes the current education system.

This pursuit of mediocrity is rooted in the belief of meritocracy. Coined by the British sociologist Michael Young in his book first published in 1958 (Young, 1959), the term *meritocracy* was meant to describe a dystopian society that assigns individuals into different occupations based on their merit, defined as intelligence and efforts and measured by IQ tests. Written as a satire, Young intended to use the book to warn against such a society (Young, 2001). Unfortunately, much to the chagrin of its creator, the term has somehow transformed from a pejorative term into a positive ideal embraced by political leaders and the general public (Allen, 2011; Celarent, 2009; Lemann, 2000; Young, 2001).

The appeal of meritocracy stems from its ostensible fairness and justness (Allen, 2011). In a meritocratic system, individuals are rewarded for their own merits (Sen, 2000), and social stratification is based on individual ability and efforts (Allen, 2011; Kaus, 1992; Young, 2001) rather than inheritance. It promises to give everyone a fair chance for social ascendance if they have the ability and put in efforts.

The logic of meritocracy is built on a set of seemingly reasonable assumptions. First, the society is hierarchically organized like a pyramid, with the few people on top awarded more responsibilities, resources, and power and the masses at the bottom with fewer responsibilities and resources. Second, assuming all members of the society desire to occupy higher positions, there needs to be a fair and just way to distribute these positions. Third, all members of a society have different degrees of merit, some more and some less. Fourth, merit can be accurately measured. Fifth, people can be sorted according to the outcomes of merit measures. Those with higher scores deserve to be at the top with more resources and more responsibilities, while those with lower scores should stay at the bottom.

In practice, many societies use schooling to implement meritocracy, and thus schools operate as a meritocracy as well. Standardized test scores such as IQ and SAT are used to grant or deny access to educational opportunities ranging from different levels of universities to talented and gifted programs in schools (Lemann, 2000). Higher scores are interpreted as having more merit and thus awarded better opportunities such as more advanced studies (college and graduate school) and more prestigious universities. Lower scores are viewed as having less merit and are accordingly denied access to more educational opportunities.

Education credentials or different levels of education attainment are used as the primary determinant in the distribution of jobs and income (Collins, 1979; Fallows, 1989; Kaus, 1992). It is standard practice that different jobs require different levels of education, and jobs requiring higher levels of education often pay more. Thus, those who are denied access to advanced education are also denied access to higher paying jobs. It is no surprise that income is closely associated with levels of education. Furthermore, the prestige of higher education institutions is also a major factor in hiring practices, with those who have access to more prestigious institutions favored for more prestigious jobs.

Therefore, in order to succeed in a meritocracy, to be placed higher on the hierarchy, one needs to demonstrate more merit than others. Merit is often measured with standardized tests, so doing well on these tests naturally becomes the goal of most students and parents. Since the reputation of educational institutions is largely determined by how well their students do on tests, teachers and school leaders also work hard to ensure their students perform well. Thus, the entire education industry is about producing excellent test scores or improving the merit of students.

As such, meritocracy leads to an ambitious, all-out pursuit of mediocrity in a number of ways. First, most standardized tests used to judge merit report a single score. These tests are typically norm-referenced, which means all students are judged against each other. In other words, one's merit is always relative to others. Those with higher scores are deemed to have more merit than those with lower scores. Thus, no matter how much merit a student actually possesses, his or her merit is defined by how well other students do on the same test. Norm-referenced tests dictate that no students can achieve at higher levels without others achieving at lower levels. Thus, it is mathematically impossible for all children to be excellent, or even above the average. In fact, half of the students are below average and only a very small percentage (about 3 percent) of students are considered "very superior." This is why only about 3 percent of eleventh graders qualify for the National Merit Scholarship Program each year. As a result, most students are deemed mediocre, no matter how hard they try or how much they know. It is not possible for all to be great, nor is it necessary, as long as one can be better than a sufficient number of others in the same group.

Second, a test, regardless of its quality, only assesses a student's ability in taking the test, that is, giving predetermined answers to predetermined questions in predetermined ways. The result of a test is one's ability measured by the test. It cannot measure anything beyond the test. As Dr. Hugh Morrison of Queen's University Belfast argues, "[M]athematical ability, indeed any ability, is not an intrinsic property of the individual; rather, it's a joint property of the individual and the measuring instrument" (Morrison, 2013). Thus, suppose Albert Einstein took a high school physics exam. The best he could do is the highest score on this test. But we cannot say that Einstein's ability in physics is the same as a high school student who also scored the highest on the same test. It is just like using a scale that ranges from 50 to 100 lbs. to weigh a 300-lb. object; the result is that the 300-lb. object weighs the same as a 100-lb. object. Thus, no test can measure true greatness or excellence, which gives no reason for students to become better than what is required to achieve a good score on a test. Even the top-scoring students are not great compared to what they could achieve.

Third, merit is limited to one's ability and interest in performing well on tests in a few subjects, primarily language, math, science, and social sciences. But not all students are born equally interested or strong in these areas, nor are they born with the same opportunities to develop abilities in these areas. As a result, some students are born with an advantage over others, thus contradicting the defining assumption of meritocracy: Merit is not hereditary. Student academic achievement has been shown to be closely associated with family backgrounds.

More important, the narrow definition of merit directs educational resources to developing only those abilities viewed as meritorious. Students who may be otherwise talented are often treated as failures and needing remediation. Their talents and passions are never supported. These students could become great in their own ways, but they never get the opportunity and thus become, at best, mediocre.

SUMMARY

The current education paradigm, rooted in the blind belief in meritocracy, does not encourage, inspire, or support individuals to become great in their own ways. Instead, it produces mediocrity by aggressively and actively pushing all students to achieve so-called academic excellence, which is impossible given how meritocracy functions today. As a result, it victimizes passion, denies greatness, and manufactures failures in students.

More importantly, meritocracy-driven education today instills a number of beliefs in parents, students, educators, and the public against the development of passions and strengths:

- Not all children can be great. A narrow definition of merit and the norm-referenced approach make it clear that some children must be worse than others. It is impossible for all children to be above the average. As a result, some parents and educators hold low expectations for some children. Some children even have low ambitions and give up early.

- Not all talents are worth developing. All children are talented in different ways, but the narrow definition of merit tells parents, educators, and children that talents outside the academic subjects tested as merit are not worth developing.

- Not all passions are worth supporting. Children can be passionate about different things, but quite often schools tell them that not all their passions are valuable or useful. Parents and educators also believe that only passions for achieving the narrowly defined merit are worth supporting and encouraging.

These beliefs may have been true in the past but not any longer because the world today needs and can use all talents (Zhao, 2009, 2012, 2016a). Furthermore, suppressing passions and not recognizing individual strengths not only damages students' confidence and self-esteem, but also leads to a waste of talents.

CHAPTER

2

All Children Are Above the Average

The Potential for Greatness

G iven the virtually non-negotiable importance attached to math in schools, parents and teachers are told constantly to make sure that students are performing at their grade level as early as preschool (Bailey, 2014). And if not, immediate remedial actions should be taken so the child does not fall behind later. Parents, teachers, and policymakers who are anxious to fix preschoolers' deficiency can take solace in the story of Jack Ma, founder of Alibaba, one of the world's largest internet companies and the largest retailer. Ma took the Chinese College Entrance Exam of the *Gaokao* in 1982. He failed to achieve the score to be admitted to college with only one point in math. That is one out of a possible score of 120 points. He tried again a year later, and this time he raised his score significantly—to 19 points. That's not good enough still. He made another attempt in 1984, and this time scored seventy-nine out of 120. Still, his total score was not high enough for even the lowest tier of four-year colleges. He ended up in a three-year program, majoring in English-Language teaching and earned a B.A. in English in 1988. Ma also applied to and was rejected by Harvard ten times.

Judging by his performance in math exams, few would have predicted that Ma would be successful in the high-tech industry, which is often believed to require a lot of math. Business should not have been his career choice, either, because it is believed to be even more math intensive. And he did not choose to study business (or perhaps was not allowed to choose given his math scores).

Jack Ma loved English, though. He began studying English at a young age in Hangzhou, one of the first Chinese cities that attracted many Western tourists in the early 1980s. He practiced English with foreign tourists by volunteering to be their tour guides around the city. He biked 40 minutes from home to an international hotel in order to practice English with foreigners. English became a great asset, and upon graduation, he became an English teacher. More importantly, his English skills put him on the launch pad to a great career. In 1995, Ma visited the United States and had his first encounter with the internet. The lack of information about beer from China and China in general inspired him to create a website, and the rest is history.

Today, Ma is one of the richest persons in Asia and 14th richest in the world. More importantly, Ma has led the revolution of retail, banking, and internet industries in China. He has created a platform for millions of ordinary Chinese to become business owners online and market their products worldwide. *Fortune* ranked him second in its 2017 World's Greatest Leaders list.

Ma's story has three important lessons. First, there is no need to fix a child's deficit too early. In fact, too much fixing too early can backfire. If it must be fixed, it can be done later. Besides Ma, there is Adam Steltzner, a "college dropout and small-town playboy (he briefly dated the model Carré Otis), an assistant manager at an organic market and an occasional grower of weed" who "had few skills and fewer prospects" but later became a NASA engineer who led the Mars Science Laboratory's EDL phase (Bilger, 2013). Steltzner struggled at school and was told by his elementary school principal that he wasn't very bright. His geometry teacher passed him with an F plus the second time he took the class just to avoid seeing him again. "His father told him he'd never amount to anything but a ditch digger" (Palca, 2012). He played rock and roll and went to music school for less than a year after high school. By any standard measure, Steltzner did not have the qualifications or perhaps talents to become a great engineer who would get a Ph.D. from CalTech and help design a Mars lander. His accomplishments as an engineer earned him membership in the prestigious Academy of Engineers in 2016.

There is also John Gurdon, the boy who was told by his headmaster that he was too stupid to study science but later won the Nobel Prize in medicine or physiology in 2012 for his pioneering work on cloning. His headmaster was wrong, but his judgment was based on solid data: John Gurdon ranked last out of 250 students in his year group at biology and in the bottom group of every other science subject when he was 15 (Collins, 2012).

Second, all children can learn, especially when it is necessary, but not all children can be great at everything. Third and most important, all children can be great at something. Ma's math, even after three years of intensive remedial work, was below average, but he definitely had the potential to be above average, even great, at something else, perhaps English and entrepreneurship.

THE LAKE WOBEGON EFFECT: (NOT SO) ILLUSIONARY SUPERIORITY

"High expectations" has become one of the most widely accepted concepts in education reforms. While it seems a great idea to hold high expectations for all children, what constitutes high expectations is not clear. For example, is the expectation that "all children learn to read by third grade" higher than the expectation that "all children can be great"? Or is the expectation that all students obtain perfect scores on the PISA—or any standardized tests, for that matter—higher than expecting all students to be great?

The answer is clear, at least to me. In both cases, the latter constitutes much higher expectations than the former. Having all children be great is without any question a much higher goal and worthier outcome than expecting all children to read by third grade or all students to obtain perfect scores on some standardized tests.

But is it possible to expect all children to be great? Is such an expectation simply a feel-good idea but completely irrational?

To start, we need a definition of great. While there are many different definitions, the one offered by the Oxford Dictionary of English works for our purposes: "of ability, quality, or eminence considerably above average." In other words, the expectation of all children being great is to expect all children to have "ability, quality, or eminence considerably above average."

Such expectation seems to be completely irrational at first sight. In fact, psychologists have uncovered a human tendency to overestimate their positive qualities (Hoorens, 1993). In some cultures such as the United States, it has been found that most people tend to believe they are better at driving, more likable, smarter, funnier, healthier, and happier than the average people. This above-the-average belief has been dubbed the Lake Wobegon Effect, after Garrison Keillor's popular humorous line describing the people in his fictional hometown Lake Wobegon, where "all the women are strong, all the men are good-looking, and all the children are above average."

This self-enhanced sense of superiority is academically known as *illusionary superiority*. It is considered illusionary because it seems impossible that most members of a given group, let alone all, can be above the group average. The intuitive assumption is that the average is the middle point of a spectrum—with half above and half below it. This assumption is only correct when the "average" means the median, or the middle value of a series of numbers. For example, if we have a group of eleven students whose scores on a math test are 100, 100, 90, 90, 90, 85, 80, 30, 30, 30, and 30, the median is 85, which means five people are above 85, and five below 85. In this case, it is not true that most people can be above the "average."

But if the "average" is the mean, which is typically what average means, the assumption is not true. In the aforementioned example, the average is 68.63, which means seven out of the eleven students are above the average and only four are below the average. That is, most of the students are above the average. It is also quite possible to have a scenario that nine out of ten can be above the average. For example, if nine students received a 50 on a math test and one received 10, the average is 46, which means nine out of the ten students are above the average, with only one below.

Thus, the finding that most people think they are above the average is not as absurd as it appears. While it is statistically impossible for all in a group to be above the average, it is actually possible for *most* people to be above the average. It is, in fact, very important to accept that most people can be above the average. For example, the view that most people cannot be healthier than the average, as has been traditionally held, has led to overdiagnosis but not necessarily improved health in general. Recent research in the medical field found that it is not absurd for most people to believe they are healthier than the average people and thus below the average risk of having certain diseases. For example, it is actually rational for most Americans to believe they are below the average risk of having lung cancer because the average cancer risk for nonsmokers is much lower than for smokers, and there are more nonsmokers than smokers. Denying this fact could lead to overdiagnosis, which has been a common problem in medicine (Vickers & Kent, 2015).

ALL CHILDREN ARE ABOVE AVERAGE: JAGGED PROFILES

While it is possible that most people can be above the average, is it possible for all to be above the average? Garrison Keillor certainly meant it as a joke, a light-hearted way to poke fun at the illusionary self-inflation tendency of some human beings. But interpreted differently, the belief that all children are above the average is not a self-enhancing illusion or some soothing chicken soup. It is actually theoretically possible for all people to be above the average. It is also practically plausible to expect everyone to become great.

The idea that it is impossible for all to be above the average is only true when a single measure is applied to a single quality. For example, all members of a group cannot be above the average in height. Someone must be below the average, although it is possible to imagine that a majority can be above the average if there are a number of people in the group who are extremely short. The same is true in other cases when using a single measure such as IQ scores or GPAs.

However, we can find that everyone in a group is above the average when multiple qualities are measured. For example, a person may be below the average in height but can easily be above the average in weight. Similarly, a person can be below the average in playing basketball, but above the average in solving math problems.

Table 2.1 shows the test scores of three hypothetical students—A, B, and C—in three subjects. A is above the average in English, B is above the average in science, and C is above the average in math. Thus, it would not be irrational to say that all three students are above the average. It is also true that all are below the average and just at the average. The reality is that each student has his or her unique profile of above-average performance in one area and below-average performance in another area, indicating their unique profiles of strengths and weaknesses. This phenomenon is called a jagged profile (Rose, 2016).

This is a jagged profile on one dimension: academic subjects. An individual's profile is not constrained to one dimension because human qualities span across many dimensions. Thus, the same can be true in other domains of human qualities. For example, Howard Gardner suggests that human beings have different profiles of intelligences (Gardner, 1983). That is, human beings are talented in different areas, with each individual varying in his or her potential ability in one or more areas. Thus, it is possible to imagine that

Table 2.1 Illustration of All Above the Average

Subject	Student			Average
	A	B	C	
English	100	0	50	50
Math	0	50	100	50
Science	50	100	0	50
Average	50	50	50	50

Student A can be extremely talented in music (100) but extremely weak in visual/spatial (5) and average in interpersonal intelligence (50). Student B can be extremely talented in visual/spatial (100), but extremely weak in interpersonal intelligence (5) and average in music (50). Student C can be extremely talented in interpersonal intelligence (100), but extremely weak in music (5) and average in visual/spatial (50). Figure 2.1 depicts this situation.

Figure 2.1 Jagged Profiles of Three Students

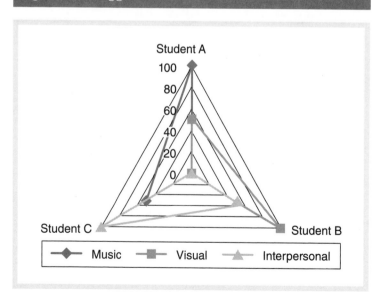

More importantly, different domains interact with each other. What makes each individual great is the result of interactions among qualities in different domains. A person's ability is at least the result of interactions between passion and talent. Taking the example of the three hypothetical students further, we can see how passion may contribute to the development of abilities. Student A is extremely talented in music, but he has zero interest in it. It is thus unlikely he would develop musical abilities to a very high level. Student C is extremely weak in musical talent but has great interest in it, so she may acquire some music skills through practice but cannot become a highly skilled musician. Student B's talent in music is only average, but he is extremely passionate about music and puts in a lot of efforts. So out of the three students, B eventually would become the best musician (see Figure 2.2).

There are many more domains that can affect the jagged profile of qualities and abilities. Individuals can vary in a multitude of domains that both affect and constitute their qualities and abilities. These domains can be both innate and experiential—more likely the interactions between the two, such as physicality, personality,

Figure 2.2 How Passion Shapes Ability

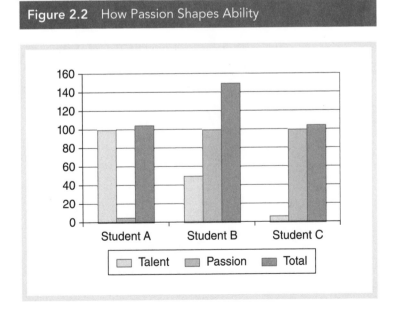

talents, opportunities, efforts, friends, and families. Each domain consists of multiple qualities across a spectrum, along which individuals vary. And these variations within a domain and combinations thereof make up a jagged profile for each individual, making everyone unique.

When everyone is a unique individual, there is no average. When there is no average, everyone can be said to be great in his or her own ways. This is why there are no two identical individuals and average persons in the world.

DOMAINS OF POTENTIAL FOR GREATNESS

Human potential for greatness can exist in a variety of areas. Humans can be great in one or more domains. It is also possible that their greatness comes from combining their potential across domains. Below are some of the known domains that contribute to the making of unique individual profiles of potential for greatness.

Physical

Human physicality varies a great deal in build, height, weight, dexterity, lung capacity, strength, and many other areas. Physical endowment is the foundation for sports activities and other physical tasks such as dancing. Different sports require different profiles of physical attributes. A good football player has a different profile from a good gymnast.

Cognitive/Talents

The cognitive domain is another source of major variations. Although there is still disagreement, the idea that human beings are differently talented instead of having one generic intelligence seems to have been generally accepted. There are different proposals about human diversity. One of the better known is Howard Gardner's theory of multiple intelligences. Despite various criticisms of the theory, it serves as a good example of how to think about strengths and weaknesses in the cognitive domain. Gardner's theory originally outlines seven areas in which individuals can have varying degrees of talent (see Table 2.2; Gardner & Hatch, 1989). Later, Gardner

Table 2.2 Gardner's Original Seven Intelligences*

Intelligence/Talent	Examples of Occupations	Core Components
Logical-mathematical	Scientist, mathematician, computer programmer, engineer	Sensitivity to, and capacity to discern, logical or numerical patterns; ability to handle long chains of reasoning
Linguistic	Poet, journalist, screen writer, actor	Sensitivity to the sounds, rhythms, and meanings of words; sensitivity to the different functions of language
Musical	Composer, violinist, DJ, singer	Ability to produce and appreciate rhythm, pitch, and timbre; appreciation of the forms of musical expressiveness
Spatial	Navigator, sculptor, virtual reality developer, video-game designer	Capacity to perceive the visual-spatial world accurately and to perform transformations on one's initial perceptions
Bodily-kinaesthetic	Dancer, athlete, physical comedian, acrobat	Ability to control one's body movements and to handle objects skillfully
Interpersonal	Therapist, salesman, customer service, life coach	Capacity to discern and respond appropriately to the moods, temperaments, motivations, and desires of other people
Intrapersonal	Psychologist, philosopher, writer, theologian	Access to one's own feelings and the ability to discriminate among them and draw accurately upon them to guide behavior; knowledge of one's own strengths, weaknesses, desires, and intelligences

*Adapted from Gardner & Hatch (1989).

suggested that other constructs, such as naturalistic, existential, and teaching-pedagogical, might be useful to include as categories of intelligence.

Daniel Pink proposes a framework that divides human capacities into left-brain-directed, or L-Directed Thinking, and right-brain-directed, or R-Directed Thinking (Pink, 2006). This framework can also be helpful for looking for strengths. According to Pink, L-Directed Thinking skills are sequential, literal, functional, textual, and analytic, which are functions believed to be performed by the left hemisphere of the human brain. The R-Directed Thinking skills are simultaneous, metaphorical, aesthetic, contextual, and synthetic, which are functions assigned to the right hemisphere of the brain. While Pink does not describe specific L-Directed Thinking skills, he provides detailed descriptions of R-Directed Thinking skills, which he believes are gaining more value (see Table 2.3).

Table 2.3 Pink's R-Directed Thinking*

Ability	Description
Design	The ability to "create something physically beautiful and emotionally transcendent."
Story	The ability to "fashion a compelling narrative."
Symphony	The ability to see "the big picture and be able to combine disparate pieces into an arresting new whole."
Empathy	The ability to "understand what makes their fellow woman or man tick, to forge relationships, and to care for others."
Play	The ability to "laugh and bring laughter to others."
Meaning	The ability to "pursue more significant desires: purpose, transcendence, and spiritual fulfillment."

*Adapted from Pink (2005, pp. 65–67).

Personality

Personality is yet another significant domain that comprises human qualities. While there are different definitions of personality, it generally refers to the characteristic patterns of thought, emotion, and behavior of individuals. The most popular theory is the Big Five Model (Goldberg, 1993). According to this model, five traits seem to capture the wide range of personalities. That is, any individual's personality is a combination of these five factors. Individuals can fall on any point on the spectrum of each factor. For example, an individual can be high on one, low on another, average on a third, and so on, which is yet another jagged profile. Table 2.4 summarizes the Big Five personality traits (Toegel & Barsoux, 2012).

Table 2.4 The Big Five Personality Traits*

Trait	Description
Openness: inventive/curious vs. consistent/cautious	The extent to which an individual is curious, open, adventurous, creative, and appreciative of novelty and variety
Conscientiousness: efficient/organized vs. easy-going/careless	The extent to which an individual tends to be organized and dependable, shows self-discipline, acts dutifully, aims for achievement, and prefers planned rather than spontaneous behavior
Extraversion: outgoing/energetic vs. solitary/reserved	The extent to which an individual seeks stimulation in the company of others; has the tendency to be talkative, energetic, assertive, and sociable; possesses positive emotions, and seeks attention
Agreeableness: friendly/compassionate vs. analytical/detached	The extent to which an individual has a tendency to be agreeable, trusting, and helpful to others, and avoids confrontation
Neuroticism: sensitive/nervous vs. secure/confident	The extent to which an individual experiences unpleasant emotions easily and is impulsive, anxious, angry, and emotionally unstable

*Adapted from Toegel & Barsoux (2012).

Passion/Intrinsic Drives

Passion is another domain in which human beings vary a great deal. People are passionate about different things. Passions are rooted in instinctual desires and basic needs. Psychologist Steven Reiss proposes that there are 16 basic needs that capture all human needs, but individuals have different combinations of them (Reiss, 2000, 2004). In other words, different people have stronger or weaker desires across these 16 areas. These basic needs can be viewed as passions, as shown in Table 2.5.

Table 2.5 Sixteen Basic Desires According to Reiss (2000, 2004)

Basic Desire	Passionate About
Acceptance	Being accepted, appreciated, and recognized; belonging
Curiosity	Exploring the unknown, knowledge, and learning
Eating	Food (finding, preparing, and enjoying food)
Family	Caring for one's children
Honor	Being truthful to their principles and faithful to cultural and traditional values and norms of one's ethnic group, family, or nation
Idealism	Social justice, altruism, equity, and fairness
Independence	Autonomy, being self-reliant, and distinct
Order	Being organized, structured, and prepared; following established rules
Physical activity	Working out, exercising the body, physical movement
Power	Leadership, taking responsibility and control, and influence over others
Romance	Sensuality, design, art, beauty, intimate relationships, and sexual relationships

(Continued)

Table 2.5 (Continued)

Basic Desire	Passionate About
Saving	Possessions, collecting and keeping things
Social contact	Relationships with others, companionship, and social acquaintances
Social status	Social significance, achievement, distinction, and elitism
Tranquility	Emotional stability, stable relations, security, calm, and protection
Vengeance	Comparing oneself to others, striking back, aggression, and retaliation

Experiences, Knowledge, and Skills

Talent, personality, and passion are the foundational sources of strengths and weaknesses, and they are enhanced or suppressed by experiences. When children come to school, what they know and are able to do vary a great deal as a result. Thus, educators can look for strengths in students' prior experiences and their knowledge and skill.

When looking for potential for greatness, it is essential to avoid applying a predetermined set of criteria to all students, particularly standards or conceptions stemming from what has been traditionally considered useful. Curriculum standards are especially to be avoided because a student's strength may lie beyond their typically narrow definition. Standardized assessments for determining interests, passions, and strengths should also be avoided because such tools (e.g., career guidance assessments) often are based on predetermined careers or professions, instead of on what students might possess.

A student's experience can be his or her potential for greatness. For example, immigrant children can have unique cross-cultural insights and appreciation for linguistic diversity. Their native language(s) is an excellent point of strength that can support the learning of another language more efficiently. The difficulties and challenges in moving between communities and cultures of immigrant children, especially those who have suffered from a multitude of hardships, may be a source of extreme flexibility, resilience, and cultural sensitivity.

Students can come to school with unique sets of skills and knowledge that are not necessarily recognized as valuable strengths, but they can be great starting points for further development. For example, a student could have developed excellent skills with and knowledge of video games or taking care of animals. These skills and knowledge may not fit in the curriculum but nonetheless can have tremendous social value for the student among his or her peers. More importantly, either can be a starting point for learning video game design, science, or other academic subjects.

Family, Community, and Social Relationships

The source of greatness goes beyond individual qualities such as talent, personality, passion, experiences, skills, and knowledge. It can also be students' social and physical contexts. Thus, when looking for the strengths of students, educators need to inquire and understand their families, communities, and social connections, as well as other resources available to them.

Students' family can help them develop strength in unique ways. For example, students whose parents are musicians or love music can have more experiences with music and thus develop a unique interest and ability in music. Likewise, those students whose parents are athletes or sports lovers can develop more interest and knowledge in sports. Similarly, students whose parents are into science, reading, math, or engineering can have more opportunities to develop knowledge and skills in these areas.

Besides parents, siblings, relatives, and even neighbors are sources of opportunities for students to develop knowledge, skills, and interests that put them above the average in unique areas. For instance, a student may have access to a neighbor who is an expert in some area or in some position to help him or her develop skills or spark an interest. Or, a student may have a brother or sister who serves as a model or mentor.

Communities can also be a source of strengths for students. Students in communities that value arts and have an abundance of artists, galleries, and art classes can have more opportunities to become interested in and better at art, for example. Likewise, communities that are rich with science museums, makerspaces, and a tinkering culture offer more opportunities for children to develop interest and strengths in science and engineering. Similarly, students living in diverse neighborhoods have more opportunities to develop an appreciation for and interest in cultural and linguistic diversity. This is why some communities are well known for producing great athletes, some for musicians, others for chefs, and still others for scientists or linguists.

Creativity

Finally, all human beings possess creativity. They are born with the ability to come up with new ideas, methods, theories, concepts, and products. They are able to transform traditional ideas, methods, and products and transcend traditional boundaries and rules. Their natural-born creativity makes it possible for human beings to create original and worthwhile products, ideas, and methods in one or more domains that set them apart. It is also possible that individuals may develop a new set of unique talents by creatively combining their average skills in different domains into something that makes them great.

To summarize, each and every student can have a combination of innate qualities and environmental experiences that helps turn him or her into a unique individual. Each student has some qualities that distinguish him or her from others, making him or her above average in some way. The key is to have a strength mindset and to look for the strengths of each child. When you look hard enough, without preconceived views, you will find them in all children.

THE AUTISTIC KID WHO BECAME GREAT WITH WORDS

Few people would call autism a blessing. As a neurodevelopmental disorder (Geschwind, 2008), autism or autism spectrum disorder negatively impacts communication and social skills. Some of the symptoms of high-functioning autism are anxiety and lower verbal reasoning ability (Sanders, 2009). Thus, it is difficult to imagine that a person who made a career out of spoken and written words and performing for large audiences on stage and radio is on the autism spectrum and called it a blessing.

That person is Garrison Keillor, the one who came up with the phrase "all the children are above average." The creator and host of the popular weekly TV show *A Prairie Home Companion* for 42 years partially credited "his gift for story to his belief that he's on the autism spectrum" (CBS News, 2016). In an interview with CBS News upon his retirement from the show in 2016, Keillor confirmed that he was "high-functioning autistic" and said he never makes eye contact.

Keillor was lucky, not only because he is on the autism spectrum, but also because he was not diagnosed as a child. So "he was allowed to be himself, a little apart. Noticing, listening . . ." (CBS News, 2016). Had he been diagnosed, the world might not have enjoyed an outstanding show for 42 years because Keillor could have been subject to intervention aimed at helping him function better. He was also lucky to have a speech teacher who taught him how to face fear of people: "If you take off your glasses, you can't see them, and they won't look like people anymore—she said they'll look like flowers on a hillside!" (CBS News, 2016).

Keillor heeded the teacher's advice and learned not to be afraid of people he cannot see. He took on broadcasting and brought us many humorous, imaginative, and poignant stories for over 40 years on radio. He also wrote novels and essays, and created fascinating characters. Among the numerous recognitions he received for his accomplishments is the Medal for Spoken Language from the American Academy of Arts and Letters in 1990, which speaks loudly about Keillor's greatness with words.

Garrison Keillor's greatness is uniquely Garrison Keillor. It is the result of the unique combination of his talents, passions, and experiences. It cannot be simply replicated, nor do others need to copy him, because everyone has the potential to be as great as Keillor, in his or her unique way. But his story compels us to ask the question, To what extent have the interventions applied to the many children with autism actually squandered their potential to become great?

CHAPTER
3

A Musician Must Make Music

The Need to Be Great

Josh helped me overcome my snake phobia. I had always been fearful of snakes, but during one of my visits to Australia, I decided I needed to get rid of this abnormal fear. While visiting Templestowe College, a secondary school in Eastern Melbourne, I was told by Principal Peter Hutton that the school has a zoo. I asked him if he could help me with my snake phobia. Peter took me to eighth grader Josh, who greeted me with warmth. He took me around the reptile room and proudly introduced me to the different kinds of snakes and lizards in various containers. Afterwards, he took out a huge python from its container and wrapped it around himself. With great confidence, he explained to me how pythons live and why they won't bite me. Then he invited me to touch the python. I obliged, albeit reluctantly. It did not feel the way I had feared. Josh then asked me to take the python and put it around my neck. Under his encouraging eyes, I did what he told me, with him holding the tail. I had the python around me for a few minutes and became completely comfortable with it. I was freed from my fear of snakes!

I told Peter how impressed I was with Josh's professional knowledge of the reptiles, confident demeanor, clear explanations, and passionate care for the animals. Peter then told me that Josh wasn't like this a year ago when he came to the school. Josh was born into a dysfunctional family and was raised by his grandmother. He was picked on all the time for his Tourette syndrome in his old school. He had very poor academic performance, very low self-esteem, and little interest in going to school. In fact, he was about to drop out of school completely when Peter, who knew Josh's grandma, invited Josh to visit Templestowe after hearing about Josh's situation.

Josh decided to move to Templestowe, mostly for its animals program. He joined the animals group because he was interested in pets. Josh took a fancy to snakes and took responsibility for caring for the snakes the school had. Because he was enjoying the snakes, he convinced his grandma to allow him to take the five or six snakes home during school holidays. Taking care of so many snakes is not easy. He had to learn how to do it—food, temperature, sanitation, and so on. He took courses about animal care and became really good with snakes. He then began to teach other students about snakes. He quickly became admired and respected by other students. He rose to become one of the leaders of the animals group in the school.

Josh also became entrepreneurial. He developed a program to charge other kids from neighboring elementary schools for teaching them how to clean the snakes and other animals. He hired a teacher from a teacher supply company to be his supervisor as he was underage as a teacher. To recruit kids from other schools for his program, he needed to learn to write and run ads in the local newspaper. "He is now confident and quite the entrepreneur," Peter updated me recently. He just won one of the ten startup grants the school offers to students annually. He invested his $2,500 startup fund in an animal breeding business. He bought a pair of breeding black-headed pythons, a very desirable exotic pet with a market price ranging from $300 to $900. The pair has already had eight babies and Josh plans to sell them.

Josh is now about to graduate from high school. He has earned his Year 12 Certificate and achieved Certificate III in animal care, which qualifies him for work with animals in industry. He also writes much better now. "He used to do lines of application," Peter told me. "His recent proposal is 12 pages long and I had to ask him for an executive summary."

What turned Josh around? What changed a boy from failure in school into a confident young entrepreneur?

It's certainly not remedial intervention programs to help with his academics—quite the contrary, it is the opportunity that allowed Josh to find his passion and strength. Following his passion and building on his strength, Josh flourished. He gained confidence from his successes, from becoming great in his own way.

Human beings not only have the potential to be great in their own unique way, but also need to be great in their own unique way. They need to be great and relevant in order to be happy, to be psychologically healthy, and to have a strong sense of self-worth. Achieving greatness matters to mental well-being and psychological health because it satisfies multiple innate needs: the need to realize one's full potential (Goldstein, 1995; Maslow, 1954; Rogers, 1961), the need for competency (White, 1959), the need for autonomy (Deci, 1975; Deci & Ryan, 1985), and the need for relationship (Baumeister & Leary, 1995).

SELF-ACTUALIZATION AND SELF-TRANSCENDENCE

Just like it is the nature of a tree to grow to its fullest potential, it is the nature of humans to realize their full potential, which has been commonly referred to as *self-actualization* by various psychologists over the past century (Goldstein, 1995; Rogers, 1961). Abraham Maslow made the term a household word through his works on human motivation in the 1950s.

Maslow places human needs on a hierarchy of five levels: physiological needs, safety needs, love and belonging, esteem, and self-actualization. In this hierarchy, lower-level needs must be satisfied in order to pursue higher-level needs. For example, humans need food, air, and water for physical survival, and thus these needs must be met before they can pursue other needs. After physiological needs are satisfied, humans are motivated by the need for safety and security such as personal safety, financial security, and health. With safety and security needs satisfied, we seek to meet the needs for love and belonging in friendship, family, and intimate relationships. Thereafter, the need for esteem, respect, and recognition takes precedence. People want to be respected, recognized, and esteemed by themselves and people with whom they are associated.

The highest level of needs is self-actualization, the desire to realize one's full potential. A person is believed to have lots of potential talents or competencies he or she could develop, but has not yet had the opportunity to do so. When lower-level needs are met, humans then have the desire (and opportunity) to uncover and develop their hidden potentials. When these potentials are realized, their need for self-actualization is gratified.

However, the need for self-actualization is fundamentally different from lower-level needs. The lower-level needs are motivations to reduce deficiency or to bridge the gap between the actual state of the individual and the desired or optimal state. For example, a person needs to maintain a certain level of sugar in his or her blood and thus needs food. But after eating, and when the sugar level in the blood is restored to its optimal state, the deficiency is reduced. The need is satisfied and diminishes.

The need for self-actualization, however, is different. Unlike the need for food, which diminishes after eating, the need for self-actualization grows as it is being met. It follows a positive-feedback loop. That is, when people uncover their hidden talents and develop them, they want to further enhance them. The better one becomes, the more he or she wants to get better. Thus, the need for self-actualization can also be called the growth need (Heylighen, 1992). The need to become better does not diminish.

In other words, self-actualization is not a fixed state, but rather a dynamic, ongoing process.

Self-actualization is key to ultimate psychological health. Only when people's profound capacities are actualized can they be truly happy and healthy mentally or be at peace with themselves: "A musician must make music; an artist must paint, a poet must write, if he is to be ultimately at peace with himself. What a man can be, he must be" (Maslow, 1954, p. 93).

Human motivation goes beyond self-actualization. In later life, Maslow added another level of motivation: self-transcendence. At this stage, people are motivated beyond the self. They "seek a benefit beyond the purely personal and seek communion with the transcendent, perhaps through mystical or transpersonal experiences; they come to identify with something greater than the purely individual self, often engaging in service to others" (Koltko-Rivera, 2006, p. 306). In other words, the ultimate motivation involves the desire not only to realize one's potential, but more importantly, to realize the potential for a purpose, for serving others and the world (Maslow, 1996).

Self-transcendent individuals seek and have peak experiences in which the self is lost, fused with the world, and integrated with others. In these experiences, the individual becomes relatively egoless. As Maslow wrote:

> As he [that is, the person in the peak experiences] gets to be more purely and singly himself he is more able to fuse with the world, with what was formerly not-self, for example, the lovers come closer to forming a unit rather than two people, the I-Thou monism becomes more possible, the creator becomes one with his work being created, the mother feels one with her child.

> That is, the greatest attainment of identity, autonomy, or selfhood is itself simultaneously a transcending of itself, a going beyond and above selfhood. The person can then become relatively egoless. (cited in Koltko-Rivera, 2006, p. 304)

Empirical research has confirmed the universal needs proposed by Maslow, although the exact arrangement of levels may not be as strict as Maslow believed (Hofstede, 1984; Tay & Diener, 2011; Wahba & Bridwell, 1976). For example, in some contexts and cultures, a lower-level need does not have to be met before seeking to satisfy higher-level needs. Nonetheless, the idea that human beings need to realize their potential and find purpose for their potential in service of others is generally accepted. The idea has been further advanced with empirical evidence uncovered by positive psychologists in recent years.

COMPETENCY, AUTONOMY, AND RELATIONSHIP

To achieve self-transcendence is to achieve authentic happiness, the state of peace with oneself. Authentic happiness comes from using one's "signature strengths and virtues in the service of something much larger than you are" (Seligman, 2002, p. 263). Thus, to achieve authentic happiness, people need to first discover and develop their potential into signature strengths and virtues (Compton & Hoffman, 2012).

Recent research in positive psychology in general and self-determination theory (SDT) in particular has contributed significantly to our understanding of how humans are naturally driven to pursue self-transcendence or authentic happiness. The need to achieve authentic happiness is underpinned by three innate psychological needs: the need for competence, the need for relatedness, and the need for autonomy (Deci & Vansteenkiste, 2004; Ryan & Deci, 2000). These needs are fundamental to all human beings. They are not learned but rather inherent. Thus, they are universally found in all human beings, regardless of culture, geographical location, gender, or race. They are like physiological needs such as the need for food and air, which are vital to the biological health of human beings.

The need for competence has to do with humans' desire to effectively deal with their environment and have an effect on it. According to SDT, rather than being passively controlled by external forces, humans are inherently proactive and "have the potential to act on and master both the inner forces (viz., their drives and emotions) and the external (i.e., environmental) forces they encounter" (Deci & Vansteenkiste, 2004, p. 23). In other words, human beings desire to learn, to become better, to have mastery experiences. The need for competence drives people toward situations that make them feel competent and away from situations that deprive them of the sense of being competent. Thus, the need for competence has been found to be strongly associated with intrinsic motivation—feedback, rewards, and communications that make people feel competent enhance their intrinsic motivation. Moreover, while efforts to increase competency by learning a new skill may initially be difficult and not necessarily enjoyable, increased competency led to more happiness and satisfaction later (Compton & Hoffman, 2012).

The need for autonomy is the universal human "urge to be causal agent, to experience volition, to act in accord with their integrated sense of self (i.e. with their interests and values), and to endorse their actions at the highest level of reflective capacity" (Deci & Vansteenkiste, 2004, p. 25). In other words, human beings desire to be autonomous, make their own decisions, and determine their own acts. Autonomy, however, does not mean independence of or isolation from others. They want a sense of "willingness and choice when acting, whether the actions are independently initiated or are in response to a request from significant others" (Deci & Vansteenkiste, 2004, p. 25). The feeling of autonomy and a lack of external coercion have been found to improve intrinsic motivation (Pink, 2009). They also improve life satisfaction through improved self-esteem, more satisfaction at work, increased persistence in working toward goals, and decreased frequency in experiences of boredom (Compton & Hoffman, 2012).

Additionally, SDT suggests that humans have the desire to experience relations with others, or "the need for mutually supportive interpersonal relationships" (Compton & Hoffman, 2012, p. 44). Every human has the "propensity to interact with, to connect to, and experience caring for other people" (Deci & Vansteenkiste, 2004, p. 25). Simply put, all human beings want to belong, interact with others, and be valuable to others. Similar to the effects of competency and autonomy, relatedness has been found to be closely associated with better psychological functioning and positive feelings or happiness. It is also related to improved motivation in learning new skills.

According to positive psychologist Martin Seligman's well-being theory, having positive relations is fundamental to the well-being of individuals. To live a fulfilling life, people need to have social relationships with others that are mutually supportive. Equally fundamental to psychological well-being is the need for accomplishment. A gratifying and fulfilling life is also dependent on a sense of competency and mastery as well as goals and challenges to strive for. In other words, human beings want more than simple happiness. They yearn to flourish. They have the desire to develop fulfilling relationships, have meaning in their lives, and master something—the desire to become great.

GREATNESS: UNIQUE WITH PURPOSE AND VALUE

To be sure, the term "greatness" is not part of the psychological literature in describing human needs and motivation. "Self-actualization," "self-transcendence," "strengths and virtues," "growth," "competence," "flourishing," and "mastery" are the words and phrases commonly used to describe the universal human tendency to become better and realize potential. The psychological literature more often than not talks about the need for self-transcendence and self-actualization, the desire for competency, and the urge for growth instead of the need for greatness.

While greatness is not explicitly stated, it is inherently implied. Greatness, as discussed in Chapter 2, means having qualities and abilities above the average, relative to others within a group. It seems impossible to have everyone actually be great; however, as previously discussed, if the group consists of only one member, he or she is automatically great. Since there are no peers to compare with, he or she is automatically peerless. Thus, to be unique is to be great.

Uniqueness is fundamental to the concept of human needs used in humanistic psychology and positive psychology. Self-actualization, for instance, is the realization of one's unique potentials. It is about becoming the best one can be. Likewise, positive psychologist Martin Seligman's discussion about strength and virtues is based on the assumption that the strengths and virtues are personal— unique to every individual. Similarly, in self-determination theory, the need for competence is people's own sense of improvement for themselves and by themselves, instead of complying with external standards or seeking standardized approval. It is entirely personal and unique. Human beings thus can be said to have the need to be great in their own way.

Humans not only have the intrinsic desire to grow, to become as great as they can be, but also they are inherently driven to turn their greatness into something valuable for others. They desire relatedness. They want to be relevant. They yearn for belonging. To construct and maintain positive social relationships, human beings need to create value for others; be a worthy partner in relationships; and make unique contributions by discovering, developing, and contributing their unique talents. As a result, the desire for relatedness or positive relationships serves as a powerful motivator that drives people to work to become great.

Likewise, the innate human need for self-transcendence, to accomplish something beyond self-satisfaction, and to live a meaningful life motivates people to become great. In order to satisfy the desire for self-transcendence, people must achieve greatness first. At the same time, striving to become great must be sustained by a desire to serve a purpose. Without a bigger purpose, people can be stuck living a life about their own material needs, or at the lower levels on Maslow's hierarchy.

THE NEED FOR GREATNESS: A SUMMARY

In summary, research in psychology shows that human beings, as an organism, are born with the need to become great. The need is natural and inherent, just like an acorn has the potential and tendency to grow into a fully flourishing oak tree. It is not learned or acquired from experiences or environments. However, experiences and environments matter. When an acorn is deprived of water, light, and nutrition, it may never become a healthy oak. Similarly, when people are deprived of opportunities to become great, they may never become what they could be. When their potential withers, they cannot live a happy, flourishing life.

The need for greatness is a potent intrinsic motivator. Just like the need for nutrition drives people into action to find food, the need for greatness drives people to learn, better their skills, and improve their abilities. More importantly, unlike the need for nutrition, which decreases as the need is met, the need for greatness grows as it is met. That is, there is no end to the need for greatness. The more we learn, the more we want to learn.

The need for greatness is universal. It exists in every member of the human species. It is not dependent on culture or other environmental factors such as family backgrounds or socioeconomic situations. It is not defined by gender or height or other cognitive or physical conditions. Every human being is endowed with the need for greatness.

THE "MENTALLY UNSTABLE" KID WHO BECAME A GREAT PSYCHOLOGIST: AN EXAMPLE

It is difficult to imagine how someone who grew up in poverty and hostility would become the psychologist who led the movement to recognize the good side of humanity. Abraham Maslow, the father of humanistic psychology, was born into a Jewish immigrant family in 1908. Maslow's early life was miserable. His parents, who emigrated from Russia, were uneducated and poor. His father was often absent physically and emotionally, and he had a mother whom he openly described as "schizophrenogenic," "ignorant," and "cruel" (Hoffman, 1988).

He faced a hostile social environment outside the home. He was persecuted and bullied by local anti-Semitic gangs because he was a Jew, and he was diagnosed as "mentally unstable." He dropped out of law school after one year, but eventually he defied all of those deficits and found his passion in psychology. He went on to become one of the greatest psychologists of the 20th century (Hoffman, 1988).

From a "mentally unstable" law school dropout to an eminent psychologist, Maslow's life exemplifies the idea that everyone has potential, even though that potential may be overlooked, under-valued, or even judged as abnormal by society. But Maslow is much more than an example. He fundamentally challenged the psychology of deficiency and shed light on the positive qualities of humanity.

Maslow broke away from the psychological tradition of Sigmund Freud. Instead of seeing the dark side of human nature and looking for sickness in human psychology as Freudian psychologists did, Maslow was optimistic about human nature. He saw the good and positive side. Rather than studying psychological illness, he devoted his life to studying the best and most positive aspects of humanity. He gave birth to the movement that studies the pursuit of happiness in psychology.

CHAPTER
4

Take Control

Personalizable
Education for Greatness

The school that transformed Josh went through a similar transformation itself. Templestowe College, hidden in the eastern
suburb of Melbourne, Australia, where plenty of high-performing
schools are located, went through ten years of continuous decline
in enrollment. When Peter Hutton took over as principal in 2009,
the school had fewer than 300 students (Preiss, 2014). It had a
horrible reputation and was about to be closed by the Victoria
government. Today, the school has become one of the most innovative schools in Australia and most desirable schools in Melbourne,
with nearly 1,000 students enrolled.

The secret to this transformation is Take Control or TC, according
to Peter Hutton. He likes the clever play on the acronym of
Templestowe College so much that he now prefers people to call
his school TC instead of Templestowe College. He certainly did TC
of TC after he arrived at this failing school. Given its failing status,

it was relatively easy for him to take control and implement sweeping changes. "Essentially their response was 'do anything, do it quickly and stop asking us,'" he was told by the teachers when he asked them how to improve the school (Preiss, 2014).

The first thing he did was against conventional wisdom or typical approaches to turning around a failing school. Instead of bringing in more discipline, standards-based intervention, data walls, monitoring of each student's progress against curriculum standards, or more homework and testing, Hutton started the transformation by asking students to take control of their own learning.

One of the most important things in learning is what to learn. To ask students to take control of their own learning should start from granting students the opportunity to study what they want to study, rather than imposing on them a curriculum predetermined by others. Thus, shortly after his arrival at TC, Hutton conducted a survey to ask the students what they would like to study if they could study anything in the world. The overwhelming responses were animals and computer game design. Hutton brought in game design studies from a local university and created the animals program. Now the school has a large animals room with all kinds of reptiles, birds, and tropical fish and two large areas for chickens, goats, and alpacas.

Over the years, the school has evolved a lot but the central theme remains the same: encouraging students to take control of their own learning. "Here they're allowed to follow their passions and interests and not just in a minor way," Hutton told a reporter from the Australian newspaper *The Age*. "They have total control, albeit signed off by their parents, to pursue their passions" (Preiss, 2014). For this purpose, TC has a "the default answer is yes" rule that says any suggestion or proposal from any student, staff, or parent has to be answered yes unless it negatively affects others or takes too much time or money.

The dramatic transformation at Templestowe made it possible for the transformation of Josh. It enabled children such as Josh to find and develop their passions and strengths so they can become great and feel valuable in their own way. This transformation is needed in all schools in order to shift from an education aimed at fixing deficits to one that supports and enhances strengths and passions so that every child can be uniquely great.

UNDERLYING BELIEFS OF PERSONALIZABLE EDUCATION

Underlying the transformation at Templestowe is the idea of personalizable education. Letting students take control of their learning requires an education that is personalizable by students, not prepersonalized for students. A personalizable education is carefully designed to encourage and enable students to create their own personal educational experiences so as to explore, experiment with, and enhance their passions and strengths.

Personalizable education is underpinned by a number of beliefs. These beliefs are derived from current understandings of human nature, the future of the world in which our children are going to live, and the educational institutions we have today. Chapters 2 and 3 discussed the theories and research supporting these beliefs in detail. These beliefs mark a fundamental departure from the underlying assumptions of traditional education in a number of significant ways.

All Children Can Become Great in Their Own Ways

As discussed in Chapter 2, each child has a unique jagged profile of qualities, abilities, and knowledge due to the interaction between nature and nurture. As a result, a child cannot be great in all areas, but he or she cannot be weak in all areas, either. A child is usually stronger in some areas and weaker in others. Traditional education focuses on improving children's weakness or fixing their deficiency in areas deemed to be important by curriculum standards, while ignoring or suppressing their strengths. Personalizable education believes that all children can be great in their unique ways and thus focuses on enhancing strengths instead of fixing deficits.

An example is the legendary UK entrepreneur Richard Branson, the "dyslexic and dunce at school" who became an entrepreneurial legend with his Virgin Group (Branson, 1998, p. 19). His headmaster told him on his last day at school that he would end up either in prison or a millionaire. As one of the 100 greatest Britons, Branson apparently fulfilled one of his headmaster's predictions.

Not as legendary yet is Chelsey, a student from a rural Ohio school who found her entrepreneurial passion and talent in a student-run business started by teacher Mark Suter. Chelsey, born to an alcoholic teenage mother and a father suffering from drug addiction, lives with her grandparents and is not the best student in the traditional sense. "She is reclusive and intentionally avoids her peers throughout the school day, and works as many hours as she can on evenings and weekends at a home improvement store to not be at home," according to teacher Mark Suter. "I didn't care about school, it was just where I had to be when I wasn't at work. I hated it," Chelsey told Mark. But then things began to change in her senior year, when Mark invited Chelsey to do something awesome, "like run-a-business-in-the-classroom awesome." She joined Grit9, a student-run web design business, via EdCorp, an education corporation supported by RealWorldScholars, a San Diego–based nonprofit organization that supports entrepreneurship education in classrooms. Chelsey talked about the change with Mark:

> When I joined Grit9, it felt like I was part of something that had meaning for me, it connects to the actual real world. Now I'm sitting in other classes trying to glean what I can from them that I can use beyond high school. I've never looked at classes like that before. Even if I don't like the class, I'm looking to see what I can get out of it. Grit9 did that. It made it all real. I want to get out of the rows of chairs, doing the same thing as every other student. This is what I needed. (M. Suter, personal communication)

All Talents Are Worth Developing

Not all talents were once economically valuable. In the Agricultural Age and early Industrial Age, for instance, only a limited spectrum of human talents had utilitarian value. Today, in the new age, a majority of traditional routine tasks that required a homogenous set of skills and knowledge are now performed by machines, and human needs have shifted from basic needs to more psychological, aesthetic, and intellectual needs thanks to the availability of more leisure time and disposable income. Thus, the full spectrum of human talents has become economically valuable (Pink, 2006; Zhao, 2012). More importantly, in the coming Fourth Industrial Revolution (Schwab, 2015) or Second Machine Age (Brynjolfsson & McAfee, 2014), developing the full spectrum of human talents has become a necessity in order for humans to compete with smart machines. Thus, while traditional education believes that only a limited spectrum of human talents (primarily academic abilities in a few subjects such as language and math) is worth developing, personalizable education must accept the idea that all human talents are worth developing.

All Children Want to Be Great and Create Value for Others

Personalizable education emphasizes trust in students. They are intrinsically motivated to improve, learn, and become great to achieve self-actualization. They are also intrinsically motivated to achieve purpose and to make genuine contributions to the world beyond themselves. They want to be accepted, respected, and valuable to others. In other words, not only do they desire to become great, but they also want to create value for others. They want to matter. Josh and Chelsey are great examples—when they can do something valuable to others, when they are allowed to create value, when they feel respected and trusted, they flourish.

All Children Are Capable of Organizing Their Own Learning

Personalizable education also follows the belief that all children are capable of managing and organizing their own learning. Sugata Mitra, one of the most prominent education scientists and a professor at Newcastle University in the United Kingdom, discovered through his well-known Computer in the Wall project that even children in the slums of India were able to learn and organize learning with a computer connected to the internet, as he discussed in a TED Talk titled "Kids Can Teach Themselves" (Mitra, 2006, 2007). He has conducted further research and expanded his experiment with self-organized learning in his School in the Cloud project (Mitra, 2012; TEDTalks, 2011). While it is almost common sense that children can learn on their own, this belief is virtually forgotten in traditional education.

FEATURES OF PERSONALIZABLE EDUCATION

Personalizable education is to encourage and enable students to take control of their own learning or build their own learning enterprise, as I wrote in my 2012 book *World Class Learners: Educating Creative and Entrepreneurial Students* (Zhao, 2012). To make education personalizable is not to let students do whatever they like whenever they like. Instead, personalizable education is carefully designed and thoughtfully implemented. High-quality personalizable education should include a set of defining features: agency, shared ownership, flexibility, and value creation.

Agency

A key feature of personalizable education is student agency. In order for students to explore, identify, and enhance their strengths and follow their passions, they must become the owners of their learning. They must have agency in designing their own learning, or, as exemplified in Templestowe College, they must take control of their own learning.

The degree of student agency varies. An easy way to think about the degree of agency a student enjoys in a school is the percentage of total school and school-related time being decided by students: that is, the proportion of time devoted to activities decided by students in consultation with adults. Traditionally, most schools require students to follow a curriculum that has been tightly prescribed, giving students no choice at all. At best, students can have some agency over how to spend their recess time and all time after school. In some education systems, even students' time after school is prescribed by education with homework and tutoring on school subjects. In these cases, the percentage of time over which students can have agency is no more than 10 percent.

While in no school can students have complete control over what they do due to resource constraints and concerns for others, the amount of time over which students can have agency can be increased significantly. For example, in Summerhill School in England and other democratic schools, students can decide what classes to attend, if at all, and in what activities they want to engage in a class. They have almost total control over how to spend their time in school as long as they follow the rules, which they have participated in making. In these schools, the percentage of time over which students can have agency would be more than 90 percent.

At Templestowe, the amount of agency is lower because of government requirements. As a government school, Templestowe must follow the curriculum sanctioned by the state government of Victoria and the federal government of Australia. It also needs to take into consideration requirements for college admissions. However, the school tried to maximize student agency. For example, it abolished year levels or grades that typically force students to study subjects prescribed based on biological age. This action allows students to choose from a much broader set of subjects that were previously out of reach because of their grade level. The school also actively solicits student suggestions for courses and projects. As a result, at Templestowe, students probably can decide about what they do for more than 70 percent of their time.

The amount of agency students can have over their time can be used as a quick measure of the personalizability of education. The higher the percentage of time students can control, the more personalizable the education is. The more personalizable the education, the more likely it is that students can develop their passions and strengths and become great. Schools wishing to teach for greatness can begin their work on increasing the amount of time over which students can have agency. Teachers can also work to increase the amount of control students can have in classes. Table 4.1 is a general guideline about the amount of time over which students have control and the quality of personalizable education.

Students' agency can vary in the different aspects of their education as well, some more consequential than others, while any kind of agency is better than no agency at all. For example, allowing students to decide which after-school club they want to join is not as consequential as enabling them to decide what classes they want to take in terms of supporting students pursuing their strengths and passions. Likewise, granting students freedom in choosing the color of their pencils is not nearly as consequential as letting them choose which books they want to read in a language class. Allowing students to decide what they can wear to school is perhaps not as consequential as allowing them to develop their courses.

Student agency can be granted on different levels. At the highest level, students can make decisions about their learning without constraints of grade levels, age, compulsory courses, or compulsory activities. Students can decide what they want to study, when they want to study it, and how they demonstrate their learning outcomes. They can choose to take tests or not, such as in Summerhill School. A lower level of agency can happen at the grade level. That

Table 4.1	Student Agency and Quality of Personalizable Education
Amount of School-Related Time Over Which Student Has Control	**Quality of Personalizable Education**
90% and above	Outstanding (Level V)
70% to 89%	Excellent (Level IV)
50% to 69%	Good (Level III)
30% to 49%	Needs Improving (Level II)
Below 30%	Poor (Level I)

is, students are still grouped based on age and are given a group of courses they must take for a given grade, but they can choose what courses to take. Agency can also be granted in a course, where teachers can allow students to suggest topics and learning materials, decide forms of assessment, and decide the pace of progress.

Shared Ownership

Another defining feature of personalizable education is shared ownership. Adults and students in a school are co-owners of the school and what happens in the school. Shared ownership is a way for students to have agency over their educational experiences by being able to contribute to and take responsibility for the culture, infrastructure, and resources in a school. Moreover, in a shared ownership school, students are not only concerned about their own interests but also the interests of others and the community as a whole.

Shared ownership is a form of broad-based ownership that has been proposed as an effective way to achieve a healthy and equitable community, business development, and job creation (Blasi, Freeman, & Kruse, 2014; Kelly, Dubb, & Duncan, 2016). In recent years, there is growing recognition of the benefits of employee-owned businesses and community-owned institutions such as banks and grocery stores (Alperovitz, 2005; Blasi et al., 2014; Kelly et al., 2016). Research suggests that broad-based ownership leads to healthier and more balanced growth and development as well as more equity.

In education, shared ownership has rarely been practiced. In traditional education, the school is owned and thus governed by adults. In the majority of schools worldwide, students have little ownership of the most important elements of the institution where they spend the majority of their time and are the very reason for which the institution exists. The curriculum is owned by the adults, as are the facilities, the rules, the activities and events, and the books in schools.

Shared ownership means shared responsibility. Personalizable education is not only about student agency, but also about student responsibility. Students, when granted the right to take control, are simultaneously expected to accept the responsibility of their actions and decisions. Not only are they expected to live with the consequences on themselves but also with those on others and the school.

Shared ownership should be established for all aspects of a school related to students' educational experiences. Of course, the first is the curriculum. In personalizable education, while students have the right to craft their own education experiences guided by their strengths and passions, their choices of courses and other learning activities are rooted in what is offered in the school. Thus, what is offered in a school is a community asset that affects everyone in the community. Students and adults, as co-owners, should bear the responsibility for increasing the quality and quantity of this community asset with their own contributions.

Including students in curriculum committees is an effective strategy that has worked well in Templestowe College. Curriculum committees or subcommittees are bodies that make decisions about curriculum matters: what courses are offered, when, by whom, and so on. They also review the current offerings and survey students regarding courses that need to be removed or added or improved. It is very important to ensure that students are not just a token on the committee. The students should have equal rights as adults, and their opinions should count as much as the adults'.

A school's physical environment and facilities such as the library and classrooms are also important community assets that affect everyone. Students should play an active role in improving the environment and facilities. They should also be substantively involved in decisions about their uses. Templestowe's library does not have an adult librarian. Students own the space, but they have rules and are encouraged to bring books from home.

Another important asset in schools that affects everyone is the soft environment or culture of the school. Students should be actively involved in making and enforcing rules that govern the conduct of members of the entire school community, just like they do in democratic schools such as Summerhill. Furthermore, students should play a significant role in strategic planning, mission development, and major events that have an impact on school culture.

Shared ownership does not happen only at the school level. It can happen at the course level as well. For example, Beijing Academy, a new secondary school in Beijing, China, changed the ownership of field trips into shared ownership. The school makes extended culture study trips to distant places an important component of its education. Previously, the adults owned these trips; they planned where to go, how to get there, where to stay, and what to do. They bore all the responsibilities for all issues related to the trip: budgeting, safety, and content. Later, they asked students to develop and defend their proposed trips before a committee of adults and students. Students and adults thus share the ownership and, as a result, responsibilities. The trips became much easier to organize and of higher quality.

It is impossible for all students to participate in all decision making directly, especially in large schools. A representative democracy perhaps works better than a direct democracy in school settings. Instead of involving all students in all decisions, schools can establish committees, with representatives elected by students. Election, rather than appointment by adults, is very important to shared ownership because it does make all students feel they are part of the process. Of course, with today's technology, schools can consult students and parents directly through social media or websites. Students can directly vote on large issues as well.

To ensure shared ownership, schools should have bylaws that clearly describe how students can participate in the governance of the school, how they can contribute to the school, and in what areas they can participate. Schools should also have infrastructures that support shared ownership, such as election days, election offices, and mechanisms for soliciting and acting on proposals from students. Perhaps a school can offer a course about shared ownership as a way to teach democracy and citizenship through an authentic experience.

Flexibility

Personalizable education must have flexibility as a defining feature. In order to maximize room for personalization, a school needs to have maximal flexibility in response to new opportunities, emerging needs, and unexpected problems. Flexibility applies to all aspects of the school: leadership, timetable, curriculum, facilities, students, and staffing.

Flexibility is first of all a mindset. A flexibility mindset believes in the value of change and that plans, no matter how carefully thought out, will always have unexpected disruptions and/or outcomes that require change. This is particularly true with students' learning plans. A student plans to take a course, for example, but discovers that he or she is not as interested in it as expected at some point. Instead of sticking to the original plan, he or she should perhaps leave the course or negotiate with the teacher for new content. The same can be true with a school project. Students may discover that they do not have the resources or skills to complete the project as planned. Instead of viewing it as a failure, schools with the flexibility mindset would consider it a great learning opportunity by suggesting to the students that they spend time acquiring the needed resources or skills. It is also possible that while studying a course or doing a project, the students discover new interests and opportunities that are more worthy of pursuing. Flexibly minded people should abandon the old course or project and pursue the newly discovered.

To support the flexibility mindset, a school needs a culture that does not look at change as bad, poor planning, or a waste of time. The leadership and adults should view change as normal and expected. After all, learning is about change; it is about discovering passions and strengths. Flexibility needs to be codified in school rules. For example, a school can have a rule that says students can change their minds about courses three times per term.

To enable personalizable education, schools need to have flexibility built in other areas. Courses do not need to be all the same length. Some can last one week, others 18 weeks. Physical facilities need to be flexible as well. Not all rooms are of the same size. Not all desks are arranged the same way. Not all technology should be of the same kind. Not all courses have to be taught by staff; students and/or community members can lead some.

Increasing flexibility requires educators to rethink what schools and classrooms have always been. We are often constrained by what already exists without questioning why it existed. For example, many educators feel constrained by timetables and scheduling, but timetables and scheduling were created for education. They can be reimagined. Perhaps Fridays can be student-driven learning days, for example. Innovative educators have reimagined how to increase flexibility by flipping the classroom or creating genius hours. Redesigning physical spaces may be too costly, but changing how spaces are used is not. Turning libraries into makerspaces changes the uses without redoing the physical building, for example.

Value Creation

Personalizable education has another defining feature: value creation. Personalizable learning is not only about supporting students' pursuit of their passions and strengths through agency, shared ownership, and flexibility, but also about guiding students in turning their passions and strengths into something valuable. By creating something valuable, students find purpose in their learning and put in efforts to enhance their strengths. They don't just learn from others, they learn for others as well.

Product-Oriented Learning (POL), first proposed in my book *World Class Learners: Educating Creative and Entrepreneurial Students* (Zhao, 2012), is an effective pedagogical approach to support value creation. POL, or entrepreneurial project-based learning, has three basic elements: it creates authentic products, it has a sustained and disciplined process, and it is strength-based. First, all learning is aimed at producing works that have a genuine purpose and audience. Learning does not begin with a textbook or predetermined sequence of knowledge and skills. Instead, it starts with identifying problems worth solving. The outcome is not a test score, completed worksheets, or an essay to be read by the teacher. Instead, it is a meaningful product, service, or program that solves a problem for someone. It can be an art piece that someone can proudly hang on a wall in his or her office. It can also be a musical performance at a community event. It can also be soap or candles that people would buy. Of course, it can also be a course that a student teaches to other students or staff.

Authentic works need to be of high quality, and high quality comes from sustained and disciplined efforts. Thus, POL requires students to go through multiple rounds of reviewing and revision, a process of learning to improve the product and develop a growth mindset. In POL, students seek feedback from their peers, teachers, potential users of their works, and professionals outside the school. Based on the feedback, they develop more knowledge and skills needed to improve their works. Then, they revise and improve.

Being strength-based is about guiding students to discover and develop their strengths and passions. It is also about discovering and avoiding their weaknesses. Furthermore, by helping students to find and develop their strengths, POL teaches students to discover other people's strengths and collaborate with them. True collaboration is based on trading strengths and outsourcing weaknesses. Unlike traditional project-based learning that asks students to do similar things, POL suggests that members of a team perform different tasks and be responsible for different aspects of the project.

POL is designed for students to be engaged in creating value for others with their strengths, passions, and efforts. To successfully implement POL requires schools and teachers to have support structures and programs that help students identify problems worth solving, develop products, and make their products available to audiences within and outside of the school. Templestowe, for example, has a program that awards start-up funds to students through a competitive process. Real World Scholars, a U.S.-based non-profit organization that promotes entrepreneurship education, has created an online marketplace for student products that enables classes to sell their products globally.

Effective POL also requires schools and teachers to have clearly written guidelines that describe the processes and procedures for reviewing and revising proposals and products. The guidelines typically include information about how students can initiate a project, where they can get help about their idea, and how their idea can be realized, as well as information about collaboration—finding weaknesses and strengths in each other and seeking collaboration with other students to improve their products.

PERSONALIZABLE EDUCATION VERSUS PERSONALIZED LEARNING

Recent years have seen a dramatic increase in personalized learning. Personalized learning has been advocated as an effective way to address the different needs of students in education. However, personalized learning, together with its variations such as personalized instruction, customized learning, and personalized education, has become almost meaningless. Worse, it has been hijacked by commercial interests as a sales pitch to market products that do not deliver a highly mechanized education or as a euphemism for products and approaches aimed at fixing the deficits of learners judged to be "slow" and "poor" by standardized tests.

Personalizable education is fundamentally different from personalized learning, individualized learning, differentiated instruction, or customized education in a number of ways.

Fixing Deficits Versus Enhancing Strengths

Personalized learning is about fixing students' deficits. It is based on the outdated assumption that all students can and should learn the same thing, even if they need to learn at different speeds or perhaps in different ways. Thus, personalized learning is about helping students catch up with others or accelerate their progress to meet predetermined standards.

In contrast, personalizable education is about enhancing students' strengths and supporting their passions. It is rooted in the belief that all children have the potential and need to become great.

Every child has a unique profile of strengths and passions that are worth developing and supporting. Every child also has weaknesses that need to be "forgiven." If a child is not interested in or good at something, it should be avoided.

Process Versus Outcome

Personalizable education emphasizes the personalization of outcomes. It encourages and supports each and every student to discover and develop his or her unique jagged profile of knowledge, skills, and other qualities such as passions and dispositions. It affords students the resources and opportunities for them to explore and experiment with their interests and talents so as to identify and enhance their strengths. The personalization is at the outcome level. In other words, personalizable education supports students being different from each other in what they know and are able to do.

In contrast, personalized learning, individualized learning, and customized learning, as they are commonly practiced today, are often about the process of learning. The outcome is predetermined, typically, by graduation requirements or curriculum standards. Students are allowed to vary only in where, when, or how fast they want to learn, but they are not allowed to decide what they want to learn. The expected outcome is that all students master the same set of knowledge and skills. Thus, personalized learning usually happens within a particular course such as math or English. This is especially true in the currently most popular form of personalized learning—learning systems or platforms delivered or assisted by technology. This form of learning offers limited choices at very low levels such as pace, place, or timing.

To Versus By

Personalized learning is almost an oxymoron because it suggests someone has done the personalization already for students. It is a great example of Henry Ford's famous saying, "Any customer can have a car painted any color that he wants so long as it is black" (Ford & Crowther, 1922, p. 72). Although personalized learning and/or differentiated instruction advocates the idea of giving students choices, the choices are often predetermined based on preconceived theory and/or big data collected from other learners. The choices are also often limited to known patterns of learning derived from previous experiences. While students may have some agency in the process, their actions are restricted to what is offered by the personalized learning system or instructional practices.

Personalizable education assumes students are the agents of personalization. It is the students who control their education. The personalization is carried out *by* the students, under guidance from adults such as teachers, counselors, and parents.

SUMMARY

All children have the potential and need to become great. To help each child achieve his or her full potential, we need an education that starts from the child's passions and strengths, instead of prescribed skills and content. Children are born learners. They want to and are able to take control of their learning. As adults, we need to create an education that supports and helps children to take control of their education, to make education personalizable. A personalizable education gives back to students the agency of learning; makes them co-owners of the education institution; is flexible so as to accommodate changes and individual needs; and has a strong culture that celebrates value creation so students can learn to use their passions, strengths, and efforts to serve the world beyond themselves.

CHAPTER
5

Trust Me

Realizing Personalizable Education

"**T**rust me," was the answer I got when I asked Chris Aviles about what's needed to support innovation in schools. Chris works at the Fair Haven School District in New Jersey. He has a cool title: the 21st Century Skills, Technology, and Innovation Coordinator. Unlike titles such as eighth-grade math teacher or tenth-grade English teacher, which immediately tell what a person does or at least give a stereotypical impression of the job, Chris's title does not. So I asked him what he does in his job. "What is right for my kids," Chris told me.

I approached Chris for an interview because he is a celebrated teacher innovator. Chris has received kudos from various institutions and people; for example, he was one of the five Emerging Leaders recognized by the International Society for Technology in Education (ISTE) in 2016 and one of the top thirty Technologists, Transformers, and Trailblazers in education recognized by the

Center for Digital Education in 2015. His innovative teaching has been covered by local newspapers and shared in national and international conferences.

The innovation programs and projects he initiated are great examples of teaching for greatness. Chris was a high school English teacher at Barnegat High School in New Jersey. "Six years into his career, Chris decided he was done with the traditional model of school and it was time to shake things up," writes Chris on his popular website Teched Up Teacher (www.techedupteacher.com). "Chris stopped whole class instruction and started blending." This was just the beginning. Later, he brought video games to his class and, in fact, turned his classroom into a video game. He started the Be About It Project, a yearlong project that allowed the students to take action on their passions, in his English class in 2013–2014. At the beginning of the year, Chris gave his students the project without any prescription. "What they did for this project was totally up to them," reflected Chris. "They could do whatever they want, with whoever they want, whenever they want, however they want" (Aviles, 2014). The only requirement was that the students make a presentation on stage to everyone about what they did. As long as they did that, all the students got an A, regardless of the content or quality of the project. He wanted to give students the opportunity to pursue their passion, to do something they might have always wanted to do, to "not just talk about it, be about it" (Aviles, 2014). The project was a great success and written up by the media. Chris also started a student-run news show, *Bengal Buzz,* that enabled students to tell their stories of the school.

Chris was recruited to Fair Haven for his innovative teaching and given the cool title. At Fair Haven, he runs the Fair Haven Innovates program, a districtwide program for fourth to eighth graders. Among others, the Fair Haven Innovates program includes the Innovation Lab, a blended-learning shared space for fourth and fifth graders to "make for others," where students can design their own projects and pursue challenges about which they are passionate. It also includes the FH Gizmos, a student-run business that sells the products they make. Students are in charge of every aspect of running the business, from bookkeeping to marketing, from customer service to designing and developing new revenue streams, and deciding what to do with the profits. Seventh and eighth graders also run businesses.

Chris is among the many educators I have come across around the world who have begun the much-needed transformation in education from transmitting prescribed knowledge to cultivating students' passions and supporting their strengths. Mark Suter, a teacher in rural Ohio, developed an innovative after-school program that runs as a business enterprise. His students designed websites and other digital products for real clients. Mark turned his classes into global businesses where students are engaged in making and selling real products. Mark won the Henry Ford's Innovation Nation Teacher Innovator Award in 2015 for his work. Ashley Greenway, an elementary school teacher in Georgia, founded the student-run business Sugar Kids Beauty in her first-grade class. Kids made beauty scrubs and sold them online. For her work, Ashley received the 2016 Allen Distinguished Educator Award. And of course, there is Peter Hutton, the principal who transformed Templestowe College in Australia, and Larry Rosenstock, founder of High Tech High.

However, the large number of innovative educators does not change the fact that today's education, by and large, is entrenched in the old paradigm, focused on fixing deficits, and mired in the broken phony meritocracy (Zhao, 2016b). We know where education needs go, and many have proven it can be done, so why doesn't our education change in the right direction? I asked Chris and others the question, What did you need to become innovative?

"Trust me" was the response.

FORCES AGAINST PERSONALIZABLE EDUCATION

"Trust me" is a cry for autonomy and respect. Just like students who need agency, autonomy, and trust to be genuinely motivated to do great work, educators need the same to do great work and to innovate. But just like students who don't enjoy a great deal of agency and autonomy in schools, educators have not had much freedom to be innovative, either.

It may appear that a principal runs a school, but in reality, the school is run by many forces—governments, higher education institutions, examination boards, testing companies, publishers, educational technology companies, and a host of other traditional educational institutions and stakeholders. It is the same for teachers. It seems that a teacher enjoys total freedom in a classroom, but all the external forces that influence schools also occupy the classroom.

These outside forces work, intentionally or unwittingly, to perpetuate the traditional education paradigm, or are perceived to do so, for a wide range of reasons. Some forces stand to benefit from such perpetuation and actively resist any meaningful change. Some feel they have no choice but to go along. Others may desire change, but the changes they make actually lead to strengthening the traditional paradigm. Whatever the reason, the world has actually seen the traditional paradigm further fortified in recent years.

Centralization, standardization, and mechanization are the hallmarks of recent education reforms aimed at closing the achievement gaps in countries that used to allow more autonomy at the local, school, and teacher level. These countries include the United States, Australia, and the United Kingdom. Education in these countries used to be held up as the poster child of education that produces happy and well-developed children, as well as creative and entrepreneurial talents who come up with the most scientific discoveries, technological inventions, and great works in the humanities and arts, especially for countries that have traditionally had a tightly controlled education system. Education in these latter countries remains highly standardized, centralized, and mechanized, despite their efforts to make drastic changes (Zhao, 2015).

As a result, educators around the world today work in a tightly controlled environment that gives them very little freedom or incentive to deviate from tradition and make education more personalizable. The majority of educators have to follow a curriculum or curriculum standards centrally prescribed by their governments. They are held accountable to produce centrally prescribed outcomes, often through tests. They are expected by parents to ensure that their students achieve excellent results in qualification exams for colleges and/or work.

To produce the prescribed outcomes, educators are asked to follow standardized approaches. There are plenty of companies and experts to supply "evidence-based" products and services, ranging from standardized instructional methods and materials, personalized learning platforms, assessment tools, professional training, and data-analyzing tools to monitor students' progress. These products and services are often marketed as ways to improve results, which are defined as student performance on standardized tests. Thus, they further perpetuate the traditional paradigm, forcing educators to be unwilling partners along the way.

Centrally prescribed curricula and outcomes (as test scores) and standardized approaches make education more mechanical and less human. Teachers are asked to do more direct instruction and follow prescribed textbooks and standards-based pacing guides. They are also asked to assess students with standardized tools frequently and monitor every student's progress. And whenever a deviation is detected, they are told to deliver intervention. Data—really, test scores—turn education into the mechanical transmission of discrete information, rather than a long journey of cultivating the growth of humans.

In a nutshell, there are so many outside forces that shape the educational experiences of students that educators are rendered merely a messenger, a deliverer of prepackaged standardized experiences for all students, just like a FedEx delivery person whose only responsibility is to make sure the box reaches its intended recipient. In many ways, with so many outside forces defining education under the pretense of being educational experts, the educators in front of the students become the only ones who do not know education, according to some policymakers. Thus, they have to be told what to do all the time.

WHAT CAN BE DONE?

But education does not have to be like this, and it should not. As numerous education innovators have demonstrated, education can be changed. It can be made personalizable so as to help each and every student actualize his or her potential and become great. To turn pockets of success demonstrated by the courageous and innovative educators, who have done it regardless of the constraints, into a full paradigm shift for all children requires the actions of everyone involved.

Governments

Governments need to retreat from overgoverning. They are responsible for the quality of education, but overgoverning does not lead to better education. The role of the government should be about input instead of outcomes. Governments should worry about ensuring funding and equitable opportunities in education for all children, rather than prescribing the same outcomes and pathways for all students.

The best (and perhaps easiest) action governments should take is to get away from determining what, when, and where all students should be taught. They should stop efforts to develop national or statewide curricula, standards, or textbooks and mandate all schools and teachers to teach accordingly. They should stop using scores on standardized tests to evaluate teachers and schools as well.

Instead, governments should invest in educational innovations. Education is a future-oriented enterprise, but ironically, it is always backward looking. Governments always encourage scaling up past practices instead of cultivating future practices. To change the situation, they should work on incentivizing educators and schools to experiment with new educational approaches.

Education Businesses

Businesses are after profit. Education is a huge business and many profit from it. Those who profit from education by supporting and servicing the traditional education paradigm are logically unwilling to abandon their currently profitable products and services. But history has taught us that it pays to pay attention to the future, especially in the face of revolutionary changes. The horseshoe makers who insisted on making horseshoes and resisted the coming of automobiles did not make nearly as much profit as those who abandoned their horseshoes and joined the auto industry.

Education faces a revolution. It is thus advisable for education businesses—publishers, testing companies, educational technology startups, consulting firms, and so on—to eye the future or, better yet, help create the future. It would be even better if businesses, out of their concern for the future of the world and all children, ceased making products that are harmful to children and started creating products and services that support the great transformation toward personalizable education.

Parents and the Public

We know that parents and the public are genuinely concerned about the future of their children and communities. But for a variety of reasons, they have not necessarily been the strong advocates for personalizable education that they should and could. Some of them may not be aware of the reasons for the fundamental change. They may not see or care about the damages of traditional education on children, or they may believe that some collateral damages are necessary to succeed in a meritocracy. Some of them may not believe the future will require different talents and abilities, and thus change is needed. Some of them may be aware of the changes but are unwilling to push for them for fear of putting their children at risk of losing the competition in the current game of education. Some may want the change but feel powerless before the giant of the traditional education empire.

Parents and the public can become better informed of the reasons for change. Schools and governments can play a significant role in this endeavor, as can the media and education scholars. More importantly, those parents and public citizens who understand the need for change can actually change public policy. They should be more active in advocating for the changes with their votes and the public discourse.

Higher Education

Higher education has always been one of the major forces that shapes K–12 education in three significant ways. First, its admissions requirements have had a defining influence on what and how schools teach because preparing students to enter higher education has been an important, if not exclusive, mission of many schools. Second, higher education prepares the workforce for schools. What kind of educators—teachers and administrators of schools—higher education prepares can significantly affect the educational experiences of students. Third, higher education institutions also are the largest producers of educational research and researchers. While educational research in general has not had sweeping influence in educational policies and practices, its influence cannot be underestimated.

Thus, higher education needs to change as well. It should change its admissions requirements and procedures, as well as become more personalizable. Educator preparation should also change in order to prepare educators to lead personalizable education. Furthermore, educational research should be more concerned about how to invent personalizable education instead of focusing on how to improve the outdated education paradigm.

Educators

To be sure, not all educators are equally willing and able to shift toward personalizable education. Despite all the constraints placed on them, if they are courageous and capable, they can still innovate. As has been demonstrated by the many education innovators around the world, changes are possible, even in the most tightly controlled places.

Personalizable education requires teachers to develop different qualities from what is required in traditional teaching. As the role of the teacher shifts from the primary or sole source of knowledge and instruction to one that mentors, coaches, and supports individual growth of students in a community, a certain set of qualities becomes more important than knowledge of content and pedagogy (Zhao, in press). In an upcoming chapter for the *Handbook on Teaching and Learning* (Hall et al., in press), I suggest a set of qualities important for teachers to have in order to support personalizable education.

Ability to identify strengths and passions. In personalizable education, it is believed that every student has strengths and passions. The child cannot be defined by prescribed standards or standardized tests. It is the teacher's responsibility to help each child explore and identify his or her strengths. Therefore, teachers must have the ability to look beyond the weaknesses and find strengths in students, as well as to create opportunities for students to develop their strengths and encourage them to follow their passions.

Ability to inspire and challenge. In personalizable education, every student is assumed to be exceptional in his or her own way. Teachers need to hold high expectations for all students. Thus, teachers should have confidence in their students and make that confidence known to them. In other words, teachers should have the ability to inspire great confidence in their students. They can motivate and challenge their students to tackle difficult tasks and persevere in the face of setbacks.

Empathy and emotional intelligence. Empathy is the ability to identify and understand others' feelings and situations. In personalizable education, students are considered individual human beings with diverse experiences and backgrounds. Teachers need empathy and emotional intelligence in order to reach each and every unique student and help him or her grow. Teachers can identify with students and understand their passions, motivations, concerns, worries, hopes, and expectations from the students' perspectives instead of imposing their own perspectives and feelings on their students.

A broad and long-term perspective of education. In personalizable education, teaching is more about the development of human qualities than the immediate acquisition of knowledge. It thus requires teachers to have a broad perspective of education, focusing more on long-term educational outcomes than short-term instructional outcomes (Zhao, 2016a). They pay more attention to educating the whole child than transmitting the content.

Management and leadership skills. In personalizable education, teachers need to move beyond classroom management. Teachers need to manage many student projects, monitor individual learning plans and pathways for each student, and lead product-oriented learning communities. Thus, teachers should have an extensive set of management and leadership skills that includes planning, communication, delegation, evaluation, and motivation.

Resourcefulness and collaboration. Teaching in personalizable education may not require as much knowledge of content and pedagogy in the traditional sense, but it does require teachers to be much more resourceful. They need to become informed of opportunities, tools, and other resources that can be made available to students, and they need to be able to identify, scrutinize, and organize these resources. Moreover, teachers need to be able to help students learn to develop and manage their own learning. Furthermore, when teaching as a community, teachers need to have strong abilities to work with their colleagues and experts outside the school.

SUMMARY: GARDEN VERSUS NATURE RESERVE

Traditional education is like gardening in which only those species deemed to have the qualities of a beautiful garden are cultivated, while those species that are deemed not as beautiful are purged as early as possible. There were good reasons to make schools gardens because not all talents and passions were valuable plants that contributed to the beauty of the garden. But today, the world has changed. As people gradually recognize the value of biodiversity for environmental sustainability and productivity, protecting every species in an ecosystem has become increasingly accepted. Instead of purging some species and cultivating others, as in a garden, nature reserves have become increasingly popular practices. Hopefully, education will soon make a similar shift, transforming gardens into nature reserves.

A word of caution is needed. Teaching for greatness does not mean pigeonholing students into a profession or vocation at a young age. It is not about only teaching to students' strengths or interests. It is really about a broad and flexible education for students to explore, experiment with, and enhance their strengths and passions. It is about *not* focusing on fixing their deficits as determined by external standards and tests.

References

Allen, A. (2011). Michael Young's *The rise of the meritocracy*: A philosophical critique. *British Journal of Educational Studies, 59*(4), 367–382.

Alperovitz, G. (2005). *America beyond capitalism: Reclaiming our wealth, our liberty, and our democracy*. Hoboken, NJ: Wiley.

Annie E. Casey Foundation. (2010). *Early warning: Why reading by the end of third grade matters*. Retrieved from http://www.aecf.org/m/resourcedoc/AECF-Early_Warning_Full_Report-2010.pdf

Annie E. Casey Foundation. (2013). *Early warning confirmed: A research update on third grade reading*. Retrieved from http://www.aecf.org/m/resourcedoc/AECF-EarlyWarningConfirmed-2013.pdf

Aviles, C. (2014, June 13). *Don't just talk about it . . .* Retrieved from http://www.techedupteacher.com/dont-just-talk-about-it/

Bailey, D. H. (2014, November 13). *What's the point of teaching math in pre-school?* Retrieved from https://www.brookings.edu/research/whats-the-point-of-teaching-math-in-preschool/

Bailey, M. J., & Dynaski, S. M. (2011). Inequality in postsecondary education. In G. J. Duncan & R. J. Murnane (Eds.), *Whither opportunity? Rising inequality, schools, and children's life chances* (pp. 117–132). New York/Chicago: Russell Sage Foundation/Spencer Foundation.

Baumeister, R. F., & Leary, M. R. (1995). The need to belong: Desire for interpersonal attachments as a fundamental human motivation. *Psychological Bulletin, 117*(3), 497–529.

Bilger, B. (2013, April 22). *The Martian chroniclers: A new era in planetary exploration.* Retrieved from http://www.newyorker.com/magazine/2013/04/22/the-martian-chroniclers

Blasi, J. R., Freeman, R. B., & Kruse, D. (2014). *The citizen's share: Reducing inequality in the 21st century* (Paperback ed.). New Haven, CT: Yale University Press.

Branson, R. (1998, September 11). "At school I was dyslexic and a dunce." *The Times* (London), p. 19.

Brynjolfsson, E., & McAfee, A. (2014). *The second machine age: Work, progress, and prosperity in a time of brilliant technologies.* New York: Norton.

Carter, P. L., & Welner, K. G. (Eds.). (2013). *Closing the opportunity gap: What America must do to give every child an even chance.* New York: Oxford University Press.

CBS News. (2016, June 26). *Garrison Keillor signs off.* Retrieved from http://www.cbsnews.com/news/garrison-keillor-signs-off/

Celarent, B. (2009). *The rise of the meritocracy, 1870–2033* by Michael Young. *American Journal of Sociology, 115*(1), 322–326.

Clark, L. (2014, November 5). *My daughter, my beautiful failure.* Retrieved from https://www.theguardian.com/commentisfree/2014/nov/05/my-daughter-my-beautiful-failure

Clark, L. (2016). *Beautiful failures: How the quest for success is harming our kids.* Sydney, Australia: Penguin Random House Australia.

Collins, N. (2012, October 8). *Sir John Gurdon, Nobel Prize winner, was "too stupid" for science at school.* Retrieved from http://www.telegraph.co.uk/news/science/science-news/9594351/Sir-John-Gurdon-Nobel-Prize-winner-was-too-stupid-for-science-at-school.html

Collins, R. (1979). *The credential society: An historical sociology of education and stratification.* New York: Academic Press.

Compton, W. C., & Hoffman, E. (2012). *Positive psychology: The science of human flourishing* (2nd ed.). Belmont, CA: Wadsworth.

Coyle, D. (2009). *The talent code: Greatness isn't born. It's grown. Here's how.* New York: Bantam.

Cross, B. E. (2007). Urban school achievement gap as a metaphor to conceal U.S. apartheid education. *Theory Into Practice, 46*(3), 247–255.

Curran, F. C., & Kellogg, A. T. (2016). Understanding science achievement gaps by race/ethnicity and gender in kindergarten and first grade. *Educational Researcher, 45*(5), 273–282. doi:10.3102/0013189X16656611

Deci, E. L. (1975). *Intrinsic motivation.* New York: Plenum.

Deci, E. L., & Ryan, R. M. (1985). *Intrinsic motivation and self-determination in human behavior.* New York: Plenum.

Deci, E. L., & Vansteenkiste, M. (2004). Self-determination theory and basic need satisfaction: Understanding human development in positive psychology. *Ricerche di Psicologia, 27*(1), 23–40.

Deresiewicz, W. (2015). *Excellent sheep: The miseducation of the American elite and the way to a meaningful life.* New York: Free Press.

Duncan, G. J., & Murnane, R. J. (Eds.). (2011). *Whither opportunity? Rising inequality, schools, and children's life chances.* New York/Chicago: Russell Sage Foundation/Spencer Foundation.

Dweck, C. S. (2008). *Mindset: The new psychology of success* (Trade pbk. ed.). New York: Ballantine.

Every Student Succeeds Act, Pub. L. No. 114-95 §114 Stat. 1177 (2015–2016).

Fallows, J. M. (1989). *More like us: Making America great again*. Boston: Houghton Mifflin.

Florida, R. (2012). *The rise of the creative class: Revisited* (2nd ed.). New York: Basic Books.

Ford, H., & Crowther, S. (1922). *My life and work*. New York: Garden City Publishing.

Franklin, B. (1780). The deformed and handsome leg. In *The papers of Benjamin Franklin* (Vol. 34). Retrieved from http://franklinpapers.org/franklin//framedVolumes.jsp

Fryer, R. G., & Levitt, S. D. (2004). Understanding the Black-White test score gap in the first two years of school. *Review of Economics and Statistics, 86*(2), 447–464.

Gardner, H. (1983). *Frames of mind: The theory of multiple intelligences*. New York: Basic Books.

Gardner, H. (2006). *Multiple intelligences: New horizons* (Rev. and updated ed.). New York: Basic Books.

Gardner, H., & Hatch, T. H. (1989). Multiple intelligences go to school: Educational implications of the theory of multiple intelligences. *Educational Researcher, 18*(8), 4–10.

Geschwind, D. H. (2008). Autism: Many genes, common pathways? *Cell, 135*(3), 391–395. doi:10.1016/j.cell.2008.10.016

Gladwell, M. (2008). *Outliers: The story of success* (Large print ed.). New York: Little, Brown.

Gleason, D. L. (2017). *At what cost? Defending adolescent development in fiercely competitive schools*. Raleigh, NC: Lulu Press.

Goldberg, L. R. (1993). The structure of phenotypic personality traits. *American Psychologist, 48*(1), 26–34.

Goldstein, K. (1995). *The organism: A holistic approach to biology derived from pathological data in man*. New York: Zone Books.

Hall, G. E., Quinn, L. F., & Gollnick, D. M. (Eds.). (in press). *Handbook on teaching and learning*. Hoboken, NJ: Wiley.

Hess, F. M. (2011, Fall). Our achievement-gap mania. Retrieved from https://www.nationalaffairs.com/publications/detail/our-achievement-gap-mania

Heylighen, F. (1992). A cognitive-systemic reconstruction of Maslow's theory of self-actualization. *Behavioral Science, 37*(1), 39–58.

Hoffman, E. (1988). *The right to be human: A biography of Abraham Maslow*. New York: St. Martin's.

Hofstede, G. (1984). The cultural relativity of the quality of life concept. *Academy of Management Review, 9*(3), 389–398.

Hoorens, V. (1993). Self-enhancement and superiority biases in social comparison. *European Review of Social Psychology, 4*(1), 113–139. doi:10.1080/14792779343000040

Jones, L. (2013). *Minding the gap: A rhetorical history of the achievement gap.* Unpublished doctoral dissertation, Louisiana State University, Baton Rouge. Retrieved from http://etd.lsu.edu/docs/available/etd-05312013-084246/unrestricted/Dissertation.20Jun13.pdf

Kaus, M. (1992). *The end of equality.* New Republic Books/Basic Books.

Kelly, M., Dubb, S., & Duncan, V. (2016). *Broad-based ownership models as tools for job creation & community development: A guide to how community development is using broad-based ownership models to help low- and moderate-income communities.* Retrieved from http://democracycollaborative.org/content/broad-based-ownership-models-tools-job-creation-and-community-development

Koltko-Rivera, M. E. (2006). Rediscovering the later version of Maslow's hierarchy of needs: Self-transcendence and opportunities for theory, research, and unification. *Review of General Psychology, 10*(4), 302–317.

Ladson-Billings, G. (2007). Pushing past the achievement gap: An essay on the language of deficit. *Journal of Negro Education, 76*(3), 316–323.

Lemann, N. (2000). *The big test: The secret history of the American meritocracy.* New York: Farrar, Straus and Giroux.

Maslow, A. H. (1954). *Motivation and personality.* New York: Harper.

Maslow, A. H. (1996). Critique of self-actualization theory. In E. Hoffman (Ed.), *Future visions: The unpublished papers of Abraham Maslow* (pp. 26–32). Thousand Oaks, CA: Sage.

Mitra, S. (2006). *The hole in the wall: Self-organising systems in education.* New York: McGraw-Hill.

Mitra, S. (2007, July 17). *Kids can teach themselves* [Video file]. Retrieved from https://www.ted.com/talks/sugata_mitra_shows_how_kids_teach_themselves

Mitra, S. (2012). *Beyond the hole in the wall: Discover the power of self-organized learning* [Kindle version]. Retrieved from https://www.amazon.com/Beyond-Hole-Wall-Discover-Self-Organized-ebook/dp/B0070YZSFQ/ref=la_B001KCZLKQ_1_1?s=books&ie=UTF8&qid=1500419170&sr=1-1

Morrison, H. (2013, December 1). *Pisa 2012 major flaw exposed.* Retrieved from https://paceni.wordpress.com/2013/12/01/pisa-2012-major-flaw-exposed/

Nichols, S. L., & Berliner, D. C. (2007). *Collateral damage: How high-stakes testing corrupts America's schools.* Cambridge, MA: Harvard Education Press.

Nichols, S. L., & Berliner, D. C. (2008). Testing the joy out of learning. *Educational Leadership, 65*(6), 14–18.

No Child Left Behind (NCLB) Act of 2001, Pub. L. No. 107–110, §115, Stat. 1425 (2002).

Ostashevsky, L. (2016). *More than five years after adopting Common Core, Kentucky's black-white achievement gap is widening—Now the state is rolling out new ideas for closing it.* Retrieved from http://hechingerreport .org/five-years-adopting-common-core-kentuckys-black-white-achievement-gap-widening/

Palca, J. (2012, August 3). *Crazy smart: When a rocker designs a Mars lander.* Retrieved from http://www.npr.org/2012/08/03/157597270/crazy-smart-when-a-rocker-designs-a-mars-lander

Partnership for 21st Century Skills. (2007). *Framework for 21st century learning.* Retrieved from http://www.21stcenturyskills.org/documents/ frameworkflyer_072307.pdf

Pink, D. H. (2005, May). *Why the world is flat.* Retrieved from https://www .wired.com/2005/05/friedman-2/

Pink, D. H. (2006). *A whole new mind: Why right-brainers will rule the future.* New York: Riverhead.

Pink, D. H. (2009). *Drive: The surprising truth about what motivates us.* New York: Riverhead.

Plucker, J. A., Hardesty, J., & Burroughs, N. (2013). *Talents on the sidelines: Excellence gaps and America's persistent talent underclass.* Retrieved from http://webdev.education.uconn.edu/static/sites/cepa/AG/excellence 2013/Excellence-Gap-10-18-13_JP_LK.pdf

Preiss, B. (2014, September 7). *Templestowe school is a class of its own.* Retrieved from http://www.theage.com.au/victoria/templestowe-school-in-a-class-of-its-own-20140906-10c6tp.html

Reardon, S. F. (2011). The widening academic achievement gap between the rich and the poor: New evidence and possible explanations. In G. J. Duncan & R. J. Murnane (Eds.), *Whither opportunity? Rising inequality, schools, and children's life chances* (pp. 91–116). New York/Chicago: Russell Sage Foundation/Spencer Foundation.

Reiss, S. (2000). *Who am I? The 16 basic desires that motivate our behavior and define our personality.* New York: Jeremy P. Tarcher/Putnam.

Reiss, S. (2004). Multifaceted nature of intrinsic motivation: The theory of 16 basic desires. *Review of General Psychology, 8*(3), 179–183.

Ridley, M. (2003). *Nature via nurture: Genes, experience, and what makes us human.* New York: HarperCollins.

Rogers, C. R. (1961). *On becoming a person: A therapist's view of psychotherapy.* Boston: Houghton Mifflin.

Rose, T. (2016). *The end of average: How we succeed in a world that values sameness.* New York: HarperOne.

Ryan, R. M., & Deci, E. L. (2000). Self-determination theory and the facilitation of intrinsic motivation, social development, and well-being. *American Psychologist, 55*(1), 68–78.

Sanders, J. L. (2009). Qualitative or quantitative differences between Asperger's disorder and autism? Historical considerations. *Journal of Autism and Developmental Disorders, 39*(11), 1560–1567.

Schwab, K. (2015, December 12). The fourth Industrial Revolution: What it means and how to respond. *Foreign Affairs.* Retrieved from https://www.foreignaffairs.com/articles/2015-12-12/fourth-industrial-revolution

Seligman, M. E. P. (2002). *Authentic happiness: Using the new positive psychology to realize your potential for lasting fulfillment.* New York: Free Press.

Sen, A. (2000). Merit and justice. In K. Arrow, S. Bowles, & S. Durlauf (Eds.), *Meritocracy and economic inequality* (pp. 5–16). Princeton, NJ: Princeton University Press.

Smith, J. M., & Kovacs, P. E. (2011). The impact of standards-based reform on teachers: The case of "No Child Left Behind." *Teachers and Teaching: Theory and Practice, 17*(2), 201–225.

Tay, L., & Diener, E. (2011). Needs and subjective well-being around the world. *Journal of Personality and Social Psychology, 101*(2), 354–365.

TEDTalks. (2011, May 25). *Sugata Mitra: The child-driven education.* Retrieved from http://www.huffingtonpost.com/tedtalks/sugata-mitra-the-child-dr_b_708043.html

Tienken, C. H., & Zhao, Y. (2013). How common standards and standardized testing widen the opportunity gap. In P. L. Carter & K. G. Welner (Eds.), *Closing the opportunity gap: What America must do to give every child an even chance* (pp. 113–122). New York: Oxford University Press.

Toegel, G., & Barsoux, J. L. (2012). How to become a better leader. *MIT Sloan Management Review, 53*(3), 51–60.

Trilling, B., & Fadel, C. (2009). *21st century skills: Learning for life in our times.* San Francisco: Wiley.

Vickers, A. J., & Kent, D. M. (2015). The Lake Wobegon effect: Why most patients are at below-average risk. *Annals of Internal Medicine, 162*(12), 866–867.

Wagner, T. (2008). *The global achievement gap: Why even our best schools don't teach the new survival skills our children need—and what we can do about it.* New York: Basic Books.

Wagner, T. (2012). *Creating innovators: The making of young people who will change the world.* New York: Scribner.

Wahba, M. A., & Bridwell, L. G. (1976). Maslow reconsidered: A review of research on the need hierarchy theory. *Organizational Behavior and Human Performance, 15*(2), 212–240.

Wang, G. (2017, June 3). *Ta 16 Sui Kaoru Hagongda Zhuanyan Shuxue 20 Duo Nian Hou Fangqi Rujin Shenghuo Nan Zili (He Entered Harbin Institute of Technology at 16, After Doing Math Research for More Than 20 Years and Gave Up Can Barely Make a Living Today).* Retrieved from http://www.yangtse.com/jiaoyu/2017-06-03/1261940.html

White, R. W. (1959). Motivation reconsidered: The concept of competence. *Psychological Review, 66*(5), 297–333.

Wong, V. C., Wing, C., & Martin, D. (2016, Spring). *Do schools respond to pressure? Evidence from NCLB implementation details.* Paper presented at Lost in Translation: Building Pathways From Knowledge to Action, Washington, DC. Evanston, IL: Society for Research on Educational Effectiveness.

World Economic Forum. (2016). *The future of jobs: Employment, skills and workforce strategy for the fourth Industrial Revolution.* Retrieved from http://www3.weforum.org/docs/WEF_Future_of_Jobs.pdf

Young, M. D. (1959). *The rise of the meritocracy, 1870–2033: The new elite of our social revolution.* New York: Random House.

Young, M. D. (2001, June 28). *Down with meritocracy, commentary.* Retrieved from http://www.theguardian.com/politics/2001/jun/29/comment

Zhao, Y. (2009). *Catching up or leading the way: American education in the age of globalization.* Alexandria, VA: ASCD.

Zhao, Y. (2012). *World class learners: Educating creative and entrepreneurial students.* Thousand Oaks, CA: Corwin.

Zhao, Y. (2015). *Lessons that matter: What we should learn from Asian school systems.* Retrieved from http://www.mitchellinstitute.org.au/reports/lessons-that-matter-what-should-we-learn-from-asias-school-systems/

Zhao, Y. (2016a). *Counting what counts: Reframing education outcomes.* Bloomington, IN: Solution Tree Press.

Zhao, Y. (2016b). From deficiency to strength: Shifting the mindset about education inequality. *Journal of Social Issues, 72*(4), 716–735.

Zhao, Y. (in press). Rethinking teacher quality in the age of smart machines. In G. E. Hall, L. F. Quinn, & D. M. Gollnick (Eds.), *Handbook on teaching and learning.* Hoboken, NJ: Wiley.

Index

blended learning, 72
personalized learning, 67–69
process of, 68
project-based learning, 66
Project-Oriented Learning,
65–67
student management of, 57–58
Leary, M. R., 43
Left-brain-directed thinking, 33
Lemann, N., 19
Levitt, S. D., 3
Liu, Hanqing, 11–14, 18

Ma, Jack, 23–24
Management, 80
Martin, D., 3
Maslow, Abraham, 43–44, 45,
50–51
Math, 23–24
McAfee, A., 57
Mechanization, of education,
74–75
Mediocrity, 18–22
Merit, 18–22
Meritocracy, 18, 73, 77
effects on students, 22
logic of, 19
mediocrity and, 20
schools as, 19
standardized tests and, 20
use of school to
implement, 19
Minority students
deficit mindset and, 4
gaps and, 2, 3
See also Privilege
Mitra, Sugata, 57–58
Morrison, Hugh, 21
Motivation, 43, 45, 50
intrinsic, 47
need for, 49

Murnane, R. J., 3
"My Daughter, My Beautiful
Failure" (Clark), 15–17

National Merit Scholarship
Program, 20
NCLB (No Child Left Behind Act),
2, 3–4
Needs, 35, 43, 44, 46
Nichols, S. L., 3
No Child Left Behind Act (NCLB),
2, 3–4

Opportunities, 7, 19–20, 37–38
Ostashevsky, L., 3
Outcomes, prescribed, 75
Outliers (Gladwell), 5–6
Overdiagnosis, 27
Ownership, shared, 61–63

Pace, 2
Palca, J., 25
Parents, 77–78
Partnership for 21st Century
Skills, 9
Passion/intrinsic domain, 35
Passions, 22, 35–36 (table)
ability and, 30, 30 (figure)
assessments for determining, 36
beliefs about, 22
curtailing, 16–18
focus on, 66, 67
greatness and, 9
identifying, 79
pursuing, 11–14
suppression of, 17–18
victimizing of, 22
Personality domain, 34
Personalized learning, 67–69
Physical domain, 31
Pink, Daniel, 9, 33, 47, 57

C⦿RWIN
LEADERSHIP

Leadership that Makes an Impact

A SAGE Publishing Company

CORWIN HAS ONE MISSION: to enhance education through intentional professional learning.

We build long-term relationships with our authors, educators, clients, and associations who partner with us to develop and continuously improve the best evidence-based practices that establish and support lifelong learning.

Solutions you want. Experts you trust. Results you need.

Author Consulting

AUTHOR CONSULTING

On-site professional learning with sustainable results! Let us help you design a professional learning plan to meet the unique needs of your school or district. www.corwin.com/pd

Institutes

INSTITUTES

Corwin Institutes provide collaborative learning experiences that equip your team with tools and action plans ready for immediate implementation. www.corwin.com/institutes

eCourses

ECOURSES

Practical, flexible online professional learning designed to let you go at your own pace. www.corwin.com/ecourses

Read2Earn

READ2EARN

Did you know you can earn graduate credit for reading this book? Find out how: www.corwin.com/read2earn